DIGITAL CLUSION, TEENS, AND YOUR LIBRARY

Recent titles in
Libraries Unlimited Professional Guides for Young Adult Librarians
C. Allen Nichols and Mary Anne Nichols, Series Editors

Teen Library Events: A Month-by-Month Guide
Kirsten Edwards

Merchandizing Library Materials to Young Adults
Mary Anne Nichols

Library Materials and Services for Teen Girls
Katie O'Dell

Serving Older Teens
Sheila Anderson

Thinking Outside the Book: Alternatives for Today's Teen
Library Collection
C. Allen Nichols

Serving Homeschooled Teens and Their Parents
Maureen T. Lerch and Janet Welch

Reaching Out to Religious Youth: A Guide to Services, Programs,
and Collections
L. Kay Carman

Classic Connections: Turning Teens on to Great Literature
Holly Koelling

DIGITAL INCLUSION, TEENS, AND YOUR LIBRARY

Exploring the Issues and Acting on Them

Lesley S. J. Farmer

Libraries Unlimited Professional Guides for Young Adult Librarians Series
C. Allen Nichols and Mary Anne Nichols

Westport, Connecticut · London

Library of Congress Cataloging-in-Publication Data

Farmer, Lesley S. J.
Digital inclusion, teens, and your library : exploring the issues and acting on them / Lesley S. J. Farmer.
p. cm.—(Libraries Unlimited professional guides for young adult librarians, ISSN 1532–5571)
Includes bibliographical references and index.
ISBN 1–59158–128–1 (pbk. : alk. paper)
1. Libraries and teenagers—United States. 2. Internet in young adults' libraries—United States. 3. Internet and teenagers—United States. 4. Technology and youth—United States. 5. Digital divide—United States. I. Title. II. Libraries Unlimited professional guides for young adult librarians.
Z718.5.F36 2005
027.62'6—dc22 2004063833

British Library Cataloguing in Publication Data is available.

Library of Congress Catalog Card Number: 2004063833
ISBN: 1–59158–128–1
ISSN: 1532–5571

First published in 2005

Libraries Unlimited, 88 Post Road West, Westport, CT 06881
A Member of the Greenwood Publishing Group, Inc.
www.lu.com

Printed in the United States of America

The paper used in this book complies with the Permanent Paper Standard issued by the National Information Standards Organization (Z39.48–1984).

10 9 8 7 6 5 4 3 2 1

Dedicated to all teens on the fringes of technology
and the libraries who serve them,
with special appreciation to Jane Guttman
who exemplifies such service

CONTENTS

SERIES FOREWORD

We firmly believe in young adult library services and advocate for teens whenever we can. We are proud of our association with Libraries Unlimited and Greenwood Publishing Group and grateful for their acknowledgment of the need for additional resources for teen-serving librarians. We intend for this series to fill those needs, providing useful and practical handbooks for library staff. Readers will find some theory and philosophical musings, but for the most part, this series will focus on real-life library issues with answers and suggestions for front-line librarians.

Our passion for young adult librarian services continues to reach new peaks. As we travel to present workshops on the various facets of working with teens in public libraries, we are encouraged by the desire of librarians everywhere to learn what they can do in their libraries to make teens welcome. This is a positive sign since too often libraries choose to ignore this underserved group of patrons. We hope you find this series to be a useful tool in fostering your own enthusiasm for teens.

Mary Anne Nichols
C. Allen Nichols
Series Editors

INTRODUCTION

> There is not such a cradle of democracy upon the earth as the Free Public Library, this republic of letters, where neither rank, office, nor wealth receive the slightest consideration.
>
> Andrew Carnegie (1835–1919)

Libraries serve as the bastions of civilizations. Ideally, they provide the resources needed for each and every individual to fulfill his or her destiny. In the digital age they offer open access to a world of information through technology, which has in the past decade become one its most important offerings. Libraries are potentially the most effective bridge across the digital divide.

Why is the library's technological role so important? Consider this. When you hear the phrase, "computer user," what image enters your mind? Is that person a male or a female? Is that person white, black, yellow, or brown? Is it someone who is rich or who is poor? Let's face it, the image is probably *not* that of a homeless Latina.

While personal computers are now present in more than half the homes in the United States, 46 percent of homes are still without personal computers. More specifically, 77 percent of whites use a computer at home, while only 41 percent of blacks and Hispanics do. Income also correlates with computer ownership and use (U.S. Department of Commerce, 2002). The populations left behind in the technological revolution are often the same populations that face obstacles in other areas of life—the poor, the isolated, minorities, and even to some extent, girls. Psychologist Gary Evans (2004) asserts that the often accumulative impact of multiple environmental risks (i.e., lack of access to technology and books, family instability, poor housing, unsafe neighborhoods) can cause long-lasting pathology.

And there is disparity in schools as well; although more than 99 percent of schools now have computers, 79 percent of high-poverty schools have classroom Internet connections compared with 90 percent of low-poverty schools (National Center for Education Statistics, 2003a). Likewise, Attewell's 2001 review of studies on technology use in K-12 schools found that gifted suburban students use state-of-the-art computers for deep learning and sophisticated graphics, while underachieving urban students use obsolete computers for drill-and-kill remedial programs. Differences also emerge along gender lines; while females outnumber males on the Internet, fewer girls than boys take computer classes or go into technology professions. All of this and more adds up to what has been termed the "digital divide." In other words, in technology, as in the economy, there are haves and have-nots.

Nevertheless, once teens are on the Internet, the digital divide disappears. The users' needs are the same. They want to access information, communicate, and have fun. Overall, about 45 percent of online users use e-mail, 39 percent make purchases online, and 35 percent look for health information. According to a 2003 AOL teen survey, 70 percent of teens use Instant Messaging. IM has now overtaken the telephone as a preferred communications channel for several reasons: low cost, ability to engage in several chats simultaneously, broadcasting options, and privacy from parents. Teens use IM to facilitate homework study groups as well as to share recreational interests.

DIMENSIONS OF TECHNOLOGY EQUITY

Of course, the actual picture is more complicated, and effective solutions involve more than plopping a Pentium IV inside every apartment in every housing project complex. The digital divide refers to both access and use. While computer access, in most cases with Internet connectivity, is necessary to become a computer user, it is not sufficient for computer literacy and technological competence. In determining technological equality, consider these three areas of concern:

1. access and ownership;
2. extent and type of use; and
3. knowledge and skills related to decisions and actions that involve the application of digital resources.

According to a 1999 report by the National Telecommunications and Information Administration, computer and Internet use is becoming critical for both economic and personal growth, and the gap between the technology-savvy and the technology-illiterate is growing.

For today's teens these skills are not optional, they are crucial. According to the Children's Partnership (2000), eight out of ten of the fastest-growing industries are computer related, and almost two-thirds of present-day jobs require computer skills. Moreover, as technology becomes more complex, advanced training will be needed. Professional and related jobs will grow the fastest, while low-level office jobs will decrease because of automation. Similarly, people with technology skills earn up to 43 percent more than those who do not possess such skills. Basically, people with technology skills are more likely to be employed and to have higher incomes (Bureau of Labor Statistics, 2004).

The digital divide also refers to the divide between older generations who were born before personal computers were widely available, as well as to younger "digital natives." Just as baby boomers are typically considered the first television generation, so Generation Y (born since 1980) is considered the first computer generation. The problem with this generalization is that it presupposes that today's teenagers are all tech-savvy, almost as if computer chips were preinstalled at birth. Too often, teachers assume that all K-12 students know and love technology, and are expert Web surfers. Not so. This assumption is hardest on teenage boys who want to be cool and accepted, and are expected to be skilled computer users, but who are lacking in one of the previously noted three areas.

In addition, some teenagers really are not interested in computers, and others do not want to admit that they do not know enough about computers to even decide whether they might want to be computer literate. This latter group needs the most attention because their lack of knowledge limits their potential and life choices.

Relative to technology, every community and every library is different, from needs to resources. Thus, this book is not intended as a prescriptive one-size-fits-all solution to the digital divide. Rather, it is meant to encourage thoughtful and studied attention to the issue, and to prompt appropriate actions by public and school librarians who work with teens.

THE LIBRARY'S ROLE

Where do libraries fit into this picture? Historically, libraries have served as the universities for the masses. Relative to a sense of place, libraries offer a neutral, safe learning space where resources and information are available to all, and where all ideas are welcome for discussion and contemplation.

More recently, libraries constitute an effective and efficient means for all people to have open access to worldwide resources, and to the supporting technology. Because of the library's historical role, librarians are generally more comfortable taking on the role of "digital inclusion" than with perpetuating the "digital divide." Indeed, today's libraries across the country offer free access to computers, databases, and other technological and online products.

However, even if the model of equality is fully implemented with the technology itself—access and ownership—there remains the profound issue of intellectual access. In terms of extent and type of use, the library's ability to facilitate the patron's *use* of computers has been less even. This is partly because libraries have traditionally focused more on building collections and helping patrons *consume* resources, including digital ones, than in using and *creating* digital products. Productivity software is more likely to be provided in school and academic libraries than in public libraries, primarily because of educational efforts to integrate technology into learning activities in the school environment.

In this area of concern, librarians have generally focused on information literacy as the main vehicle for helping patrons become computer literate. While technological competence may transcend the boundaries of information literacy, such as knowing how to install RAM or fix a printer, most computer skills fit within the framework of accessing, evaluating, and using information purposefully. The ability to evaluate Internet sources seems to be the main niche for libraries relative to intellectual access to technology.

To achieve the ideal of digital inclusion with young adults, you must first appreciate the complex issues facing that age group: developmental, societal, and situational. Furthermore, specific subgroups and individuals may face additional barriers to technology because of disabilities, language issues, or illiteracy. While the school curriculum is usually considered the main avenue of access—both physical and intellectual—to technology, many teens fall into educational gaps. In some cases, schools have slow Internet connections or might limit Internet access to class lab use; in other cases, technical assistance is lacking or teachers may be unprepared to integrate technology into the curriculum. Moreover, a significant percentage of teens are not participants in the traditional school system—for example, homeless teens, dropouts, migrant workers, incarcerated teens, and others. Today, along with supporting and building textual literacy, libraries are charged with supporting and building computer literacy.

Information literacy offers the key to achieving digital inclusion and computer competency because it can meet young people's specific personal and educational needs. It establishes a purposeful, teen-centric perspective rather than furthering the attitude of technology for technology's sake, which does not work well for youth who find themselves on the "wrong" side of the digital divide. And in cases where technology is perceived and used mainly for entertainment, librarians can, through resources and learning activities, help teens become lifelong learners and productive citizens.

FOSTERING DIGITAL INCLUSION

How can you maximize your impact and effectively foster digital inclusion of young adults? You must start by determining your library's role in bridging the digital divide. Technology skills and digital resources raise the issue of systemwide library commitment to digital inclusion through several initiatives: teen access to Internet-connected computers, infusion of technology across school curricula, staff development, and technical support. Technology-related library services can also become outreach opportunities to get needed resources as well as to provide the community with well-prepared future employees and current educational opportunities. Chapter 1 lays out the issues and solutions that libraries must resolve.

After that, take a good look at today's teenagers—their needs, habits, and diversity. Who are the teens who are excluded from the technological revolution? This is the question Chapter 2 addresses.

What does technology have to offer teens? We will examine the world of technology, particularly as it affects and relates to teens on the digital fringe. Studies (The Children's Partnership, 2000; Katz & Rice, 2002; Wilhelm, Carmen, & Reynolds, 2002) find low-income populations using the Internet largely for entertainment, for sharing personal information, and for self-improvement in the areas of job searching and online training. Technology has significant career and societal implications, which might not occur to young adults or to their community leaders. When libraries offer computer access and training to teens, the entire community can benefit. Chapter 3 provides some positive scenarios.

If the image of technology for marginalized teens is fast-food cash registers, then it should come to no surprise that they might not embrace technology. Chapter 4 examines teens' perception of technology, particularly relative to information and communication.

Chapter 5 addresses physical access to technology, the first hurdle to overcome in crossing the digital divide. With inequitable access in schools, and even poorer access for out-of-school teenagers, libraries as public institutions have a great responsibility to provide teens with adequate technology as well as opportunities to use it.

Even if young adults get their hands on the equipment, they might not be able to take advantage of the information resources themselves. Chapter 6 describes ways in which you can help teens become computer literate while being sensitive to developmental issues such as the different ways that young adults learn.

Literacy requires the ability to comprehend, evaluate, and use information. In some cases, teens have a specific purpose in mind; in other cases, they need to be literate in order to respond critically to societal messages. Chapter 7 offers a variety of ways to facilitate teens' intellectual access so they can control their lives to a greater degree.

Cultural values and content issues also affect digital discrepancies. Chapter 8 discusses these factors, and suggests ways to deal with these content realities, particularly through the use of community-based efforts.

How do today's teenagers use technology? How *could* they use it? Chapter 9 focuses on intellectually stimulating and creative uses of technology that engage teens now and lead to lifelong activities.

Chapter 10, which is a "call to action," outlines the principles and process of "best practice," with examples of how libraries nationwide are reaching out to the underserved. The chapter offers scenarios of real-life activities and services that can be adapted to meet local community needs.

A bibliography of cited sources and further readings concludes the book.

As major technology issues are explored in this work, the unique and vital role of libraries becomes more apparent than ever. Indeed, libraries have the potential to meet young people's technological needs, and thus enable them to face today's challenges and shape tomorrow's world.

WORKS CITED

Attewell, P. (2001, July). The first and second digital divides. *Sociology of Education, 74*(3), 252–259.

Bureau of Labor Statistics. (2004). *Tomorrow's jobs.* Washington, DC: U.S. Department of Labor.

The Children's Partnership. *Online content for low-income and underserved Americans.* (2000). Santa Monica, CA: The Children's Partnership. http://www.childrenspartnership.org/pub/low_income/index.html.

Evans, G. (2004, February). The environment of childhood poverty. *American Psychologist, 59*(2), 77–92.

Katz, J., & Rice, R. (2002). *Social consequences of Internet use: Access, involvement, and interaction.* Cambridge, MA: MIT Press.

National Center for Education Statistics. (2003). *Computer and Internet use by children and adolescents in 2001.* Washington, DC: U.S. Department of Education.

National Center for Education Statistics. (2003a). *Internet access in U.S. public schools and classrooms: 1994–2001.* Washington, DC: National Center for Education Statistics.

National Telecommunications and Information Administration. (1999). *Falling through the Net: Defining the digital divide.* Washington, DC: U.S. Department of Commerce. http://www.ntia.doc.gov/ntiahome/fttn99/contents.html.

U.S. Department of Commerce. (2002). *A nation online: How Americans are expanding their use of the Internet.* Washington, DC: U.S. Department of Commerce. http://www.ntia.doc.gov/ntiahome/dn/.

Wilhelm, T., Carmen, D., & Reynolds, M. (2002). *Connecting kids to technology: Challenges and opportunities.* Baltimore, MD: Annie E. Casey Foundation. http://www.aypf.org/forumbriefs/2002/fb071802.htm.

1

LAYING THE GROUNDWORK

For a Librarian

Give me a hand up
You have the know-how
Give me a hand up
You have the tools
Give me a hand up
From my poverty
From my hand-to-mouth life
Make a space, show me how . . .
Give me a hand up
I'll be readin' right back
When I quiet my shame and fears
When I silence my doubts and tears . . .
Give me a hand up
I don't want no hand-outs
Show me technology
And I'll show you . . .

Jane Guttman

By their nature as a public institution, libraries are a logical place to foster digital inclusion. The Library Bill of Rights mandates service to all populations, and these programs should now encompass a variety of technologies. Furthermore, libraries serve as the one public agency that offers free access to information, and helps people use that information for their own needs.

Likewise, libraries are a natural vehicle for bridging the digital divide. Even in 2001, 95 percent of all public libraries had public access to the Internet, in large part due to e-rate discounts and Gates Foundation donations. As librarians you make the largest difference, though, because you have the technological expertise and professional background to help teens choose from a "vast sea of unwashed resources out there" (Technology Counts 2001, 2001).

In helping teens to become empowered by using technology, you are pushing your social mission of education for a democratic society. In building community in response to social and individual needs, you are practicing civic librarianship (McCabe, 2001). To this end, you need to know your community—and yourselves. Then you need to leverage the library program within the context of the potential world of teen library users.

QUALITIES OF YOUTH-SERVING LIBRARIANS

Coming to the library may be a big step for teens. The preconceived notions of libraries and librarians may run counter to teen hangouts and teen idols. Images of "shh" and overdue fines may flash in their minds. Those teens who have had few experiences with technology might not think of the library as a likely techie place. Therefore, each encounter in the library should inspire a positive and welcoming picture.

Personal Qualities

While all librarians should be committed to serving all patrons, teens need to know that at least one librarian will take the time to really listen to them, address their needs, and advocate for them. In developing a trusting relationship with one dependable adult professional, teens can become more resilient as well as more competent.

So what personal qualities help make you the perfect teen-serving librarian? This list would do any professional proud, but it focuses on those dispositions that teens appreciate and need:

- active, intellectually curious, creative, self-confident, authentic
- hopeful, resilient and flexible, persistent, risk-taking and open-minded, able to take advantage of learning moments, comfortable multitasking
- mentally stable and responsible
- possessing a good sense of humor and sense of perspective
- caring and compassionate about others and themselves
- respectful and appreciative of others, collaborative
- enthusiastic about libraries and teens
- appreciative and trusting of teens, able to bond with them and advocate for them
- able to find the gift in each teen and help him/her develop it and contribute to the community (Wiles & Bondi, 1993)

No matter what your personal qualities, as a librarian you should be authentic and true to yourself; otherwise, teens will turn off immediately.

Professional Qualities

Still, liking teens and projecting a positive personality are not enough. To gain respect, youth-serving librarians need to provide the highest quality of service. The Young Adult Library Services Association (2003) has developed a detailed list of competencies for librarians serving youth, categorizing these skills into seven areas:

- leadership and professionalism
- knowledge of client group
- communication
- administration
- knowledge of materials
- access to information
- services

Here are important professional abilities that you, as a librarian, should exhibit:

- know and understand adolescent development
- know and understand school curriculum

- know and apply best practice in library science
- understand group dynamics and facilitate collaboration
- work with teens in different group arrangements
- instruct and coach taking into consideration different learning styles and intellectual needs
- read fluently and promote reading
- listen and observe actively
- provide timely feedback as needed or desired by teen
- handle high-activity, high-noise environment effectively
- handle inappropriate behavior calmly, respectfully, and positively (Wiles & Bondi, 1993)

Teen Librarian (http://www.teenlibrarian.com) offers additional resources and practical tips for working with teens.

In terms of technology, try to be as knowledgeable as possible about the subject, or at least be willing to learn about it. In some cases, teens may know more about one aspect of technology than you do, so honest appraisal is important. To be fair, though, you bring a knowledge of information and a sense of ethical behavior to the table, which shapes the use of technology in support of the social good.

Interactions with Teens

Think of skills, knowledge, and disposition as assets, and leverage these assets to optimize your work with teens. These interactions may range from a chance single question (e.g., "Where is the bathroom?") to an enduring mentoring relationship. Likewise, you may be working with a single teen, a classroom of students, or a library-related club. Regardless of the time frame, certain behaviors should be exhibited:

- respect, value, and listen to each teenager
- communicate high expectations in behavior, ability, and attitudes
- promote and reinforce positive citizenship and diversity
- engage teens' natural curiosity and creativity
- build a sense of family and community (Young Adult Library Services Association, 2003)

Be mindful of the immediate and community culture of expectations. For instance, in a school setting, if group work is assigned regularly, expect some constructive noise. If teens respond positively to a directive manner that is used by local community members, then that tack would be appropriate. The key is consistent and credible parameters in which teens can thrive.

At the beginning stage of library use, teens act like consumers, getting the resources and services they want and need. At the next stage, teens can start to contribute to the library program and actually help to shape it to their needs. The initiative may start with the teen or with you; in either case, a sense of trust must be established first. One thing is certain, though: you need to be receptive to teen wishes to get involved, even if that desire may be unspoken. You should also persevere in attracting young adults on the fringes of technology; those individuals may be more difficult to attract for several reasons: prior negative experiences with social institutions, a disconnect between their worlds and the library, peer pressure, fear of the unknown, or personal discomfort. Generally, younger teens are easier to enlist than older teens. Additionally, targeted outreach that takes advantage of existing community ties has more success. Here are some other points to remember:

- accept short-term, project-based commitments
- aim for concrete, immediate results
- build on teens' interests and skills
- agree on expectations, and train teens as needed
- thank teens for their efforts, and express how their work impacts the library
- make it comfortable for teens to change their minds

Some ways that teens can begin to get involved with technology include:

- suggesting URLs or topics that could be bookmarked on the library Web site
- suggesting guest speakers to talk about technology at the library
- identifying broken links on the library Web portal
- test the use of instruction sheets for technology programs at the library

- previewing and testing software and subscription periodical databases
- writing online reviews of books for the library Web page
- videotaping a class, workshop, or lecture at the library

If teens find that they enjoy their experience in the library, and find that they are learning skills that help them in other arenas of life, they may be candidates as library aides. This scenario is more likely in school settings, although teens may also be able to volunteer, get paid, or receive class credits (service learning) for their efforts in public libraries.

Consider recruiting teens in pairs so they will have immediate mutual support; there are pros and cons to "hiring" buddies, such as interdependence or constant distractions. Several books deal with student assistants (e.g., Bard, 1999; Braun, 2003; Farmer, 1997; O'Dell, 2002). In addition, the Young Adult Library Services Association has a Web site (http://www.ala.org/tags) and listserv (http://www.topica.com/lists/tagad-l) targeted to librarians who work with teen advisory groups. At the most basic level, you should follow these steps:

1. identify tasks that teens can perform
2. identify the skills needed to perform those tasks
3. recruit teens
4. interview teens: match interests and skills to tasks, get recommendations, set clear expectations
5. orient and train teens
6. supervise teens
7. correct and reward teens

This process helps teens build positive work habits, which for some might be a new experience, so additional attention and support is needed.

In terms of technology, a few specific reminders follow:

- Get recommendations from other teachers about the teens' capabilities, work habits, honesty, and maturity.
- Have teens demonstrate the relevant technology skill before letting them act independently.
- If teens do not have a particular technical skill, demonstrate it and the process first so teens can decide if they want to learn to do it.

- Allow peer training, but observe and supervise them at first for quality control. Better yet, train teens on how to coach their peers since technical skills differ from instructional skills.
- Encourage teens to check with an adult expert (i.e., a librarian or tech specialist) if they encounter technical problems rather than independently troubleshoot.
- Keep passwords confidential so teens will not be in an awkward position if pressured by peers to hack the system.

Because socialization is an important part of growing up, you should make sure to incorporate social activities into your work with teens. Library aides can work together and also form a library aide group. To get teens interested in technology, you can sponsor tech-related clubs in addition to and separate from a library service model. Alternatively, you can collaborate with other teachers or community groups to cosponsor such activities. Some other possibilities include:

- video club
- local cable television station community production crew
- graphics club
- Web design club
- Think Quest competition (http://www.thinkquest.com)
- Technology Student Association (http://www.tsawww.org)
- technology mentoring programs (particularly for girls)

Detailed descriptions and guidelines for representative activities are provided in Chapter 10. For most of these activities, sustained involvement greatly increases their impact, although you need to be sensitive to teens' conflicting time priorities. When they have sustained experiences, though, you can empower teens to become experts and give them opportunities to produce original work and teach others: peers, youngsters, or adults.

When you serve as a club advisor, be sure to follow the relevant institutional guidelines. Expectations need to be made clear so teens are not promised powers that they cannot carry out. Control issues must be negotiated carefully to insure respect and fairness for all parties, particularly if activities attract teens from competing social groups. Within that framework, though, remember that you are providing the safety net for teens' activities, guiding rather than pulling them along. As such, you are acting as a partner, advocate, and positive role model. Here, then, are some tips to make those clubs more meaningful and successful.

- Provide training and opportunities for teen leadership and decision making.
- Let teens develop their own goals.
- Have teens consider immediate and long-term goals with concrete evidence of success.
- Provide timely and appropriate feedback.
- Give teens opportunities to share and "show off."
- Let teens fail—and learn from their mistakes—as long as it is safe and legal.
- Provide outlets for teen energy and restlessness.
- Help develop a sense of belonging, yet allow for independent action and values.
- Integrate social activity.
- Provide food.
- Be aware of positive and negative aspects of peer pressure.
- Help teens negotiate differences and solve problems.
- Encourage benchmark celebrations and recognitions.

QUALITIES OF LIBRARIES SERVING TEENS

A supportive library staff and infrastructure is essential to the success of your work. Teen-serving public librarians, in particular, often act as advocates and liaison to the rest of the staff, but the entire library personnel and board should support your efforts and be informed of teen issues. Staff might need to become more tolerant of teen behavior and group norms and work with other library patrons to insure acceptance of all users of library resources.

In short, a positive, coordinated, and caring service for all teenagers requires attention to atmosphere as well as resources and services. In the public library, a teens-only space conveys an explicit message that teens have a stable, high-profile place; give teens a voice in developing and maintaining that area as well. Technological equity and fairness needs to be insured for teens. A bank of computers that give teens first priority, at least during peak hours of teen use, signals a caring attitude. The library should also offer a variety of programs so teens can explore their identities and build their skills.

To attract teens, libraries should be seen as active environments for learning and personal growth. Having a warehouse of equipment does not make the grade. To insure that those services and programs meet local teen needs, enlist teen participation in identifying and engaging topics and inviting presenters. Examples of appropriate services that incorporate technology include:

- homework centers and tutoring services
- venues for cultural expressions via technology: video productions, electronic music, digital publications and imaging, and so forth
- interactive telecommunications: chat, blogging, video conferencing
- technology shows and fairs
- technology career advice

Chapter 10 provides guidelines and examples of successful library programs.

Likely topics for short-term, teen-friendly programs or events that incorporate technology include, among others:

- health information: Web-based resources, videotapes and video conferencing, technology tools for diagnosing health situations
- money management and financial aid: Web-based resources, videotapes and video conferencing, spreadsheet use
- civil rights and political activism: Web-based resources, videotapes and video conferencing, telecommunications skills, publications production techniques
- computer gaming: software programs, playing and production techniques, videos and video conferencing
- entertainment: Web-based resources, videotapes and video conferencing, CDs/DVDs, production techniques using a variety of formats

Teens can also videotape live programs, and the library can circulate those tapes, so others can have access to the information.

The organization and infrastructure of the library should also give priority to teen issues. A positive vision that focuses on youth development should be developed. Policies should be established that support youth, such as fee/free services. Staff development should address ways to improve service to teens, such as:

- understanding and appreciating developmental issues
- communication with teens
- cross-cultural communication
- nonverbal communication
- dealing with different frames of reference
- learning styles
- dealing with teens on the fringes

As a best practice, join at least one teen listserv or newsgroup. In addition, encourage library staff to develop close, positive working relationships with community entities in support of youth. Indeed, sometimes library services may reach teen tech fringers primarily through the local agency or meeting place.

Regardless of the approach your library takes, be sure to assess community needs and evaluate library services on an ongoing basis to determine what direction to take and what modifications to make to insure that teens are well served. Sources of information may include:

- census information (e.g., households, demographics, income, employment)
- school information (e.g., demographics, achievement, attendance, behavior)
- community information (e.g., Chamber of Commerce, public agencies, parks and recreation centers, faith-based organizations, real estate offices, youth groups)
- local media coverage
- focus groups of teens, parents, school staff, youth-serving agencies, and community members.

Assessment tools may include records analysis (e.g., circulation statistics, Web hits, library use, meeting minutes), surveys, interviews, in-library and community observation of teens' actions, samples of their work (e.g., school projects, community service, local productions). Assessment should identify the library's contributing resources and services, and then link those inputs to teen outcomes in terms of behaviors and products. How do teens learn about the library? How many teens participate, and to what extent? What are they learning? What technological skills are being used? Do teens continue to take advantage of the library? What roles do they play? Do teens contribute more to their community? Do they stay in school? Does impact vary according to teen subgroups (e.g., gender, ethnicity, age, literacy level, economic status). Follow-up questions are often needed to ferret out the reasons for the results. Libraries should also communicate regularly with community entities to address these issues on a system-wide basis. By figuring out what works and what does not, by building on successes and overcoming obstacles, librarians can optimize their impact on teen engagement with technology.

For example, be sensitive to the resources available to technologically disadvantaged teens *outside* the library. Costs must be kept low and access must be optimized. Show teens how to get free e-mail accounts and services. Library-sponsored online resources should be made available in low-tech formats (i.e., without frames, images, or Java scripting) to maximize access. By making technology decisions based on teens' real lives and needs within the community, you demonstrate your care and acceptance of teens *as they are.*

LIBRARIES AND COMMUNITIES

The fate of teens impacts your entire community, so it makes sense that your library collaborates with local entities in order to help them succeed.

Identifying Community Collaborators

As you get to know the teens in your community, pay attention to the environment in which they exist. In the process, make sure to note the assets within the community and start to develop positive relationships with those contributors. Where do teens and families go for information and support? Likely community resources include:

- public agencies (e.g., education, health, safety)
- businesses (services, manufacturers, merchandisers)
- professional organizations

- social groups
- philanthropic groups
- cultural and entertainment groups
- recreation centers, sports
- faith-based entities
- local media

The local telephone directory and Chamber of Commerce are good starting points to get leads.

After identifying these organizations, contact youth-serving agencies in order to discuss teen issues and ways to meet their needs. In some cases, these community groups already maintain local databases that list sources of assistance and coordinate efforts to support teens, be it through resources, research, projects, expertise, policies, or advocacy. As you identify available resources and services, you can leverage them to maximize teen support.

Remember that not all community groups are created equal. Consider each group's goals, expertise, available resources, stability, support base, reputation in the community, willingness to collaborate, and its commitment to teens and technology. Find out if there are competing priorities, outside pressures, or lack of incentives that might jeopardize partnerships. When in doubt, focus on a few solid community entities rather than trying to include every group on principle.

Building Coalitions

As you begin to make contacts and build a sense of community, remember to identify your own contributions to the effort and your library's assets: a safe and neutral public space, a rich collection of information in a variety of formats, open access to technology and information worldwide, cultural and educational programs and services, literacy support, communications channels, trained professionals to help people be effective users of information and ideas, extended and convenient hours of operation, public and private funding to maintain services, and access to a broad spectrum of the community. With those assets, you can build meaningful relationships with community groups relative to issues about teens and technology in several ways:

- collecting, displaying, and disseminating local information
- developing bibliographies and other publications

- speaking to local groups
- providing background information
- training community members
- joining community groups
- providing a public meeting space
- participating, volunteering, hosting, and cosponsoring events and programs
- advocating for change (Farmer, 1994, p. 83)

As you build coalitions to address the issue of teens and technology, look for ways to deepen those relationships and approach projects on a more systematic, sustained basis. Gambone, Klem, and Connell (2002) suggest the following steps:

1. gather information
2. identify and recruit stakeholders
3. set attainable goals
4. establish evaluation criteria
5. identify resources
6. plan collaboratively
7. seek additional funding and support through grant writing and campaigns

Several factors help to maximize community coalitions: needs assessment and analysis, alignment with current structures and services, clear and ongoing communication and agreements, written policies, joint decision making, emphasis on flexibility and creativity, commitment to improve services, and follow-up on issues (Greene & Kochhar-Bryant, 2003).

Intent and planning set the stage, but cooperative efforts should be coordinated to insure sustained impact on serving teens. The following elements need to be in place and monitored:

- leadership and vision
- clear expectations, procedures, and policies
- defined roles and contributions
- individual program planning and monitoring

- information collection, storage, organization, and retrieval procedures
- adequate allocation of time, funding, staffing, and resources
- service coordination and linking
- service monitoring and follow-through
- professional development
- individual and interagency advocacy
- services evaluation and follow-up (Greene & Kochhar-Bryant, 2003)

Working with other groups requires time, effort, and ongoing negotiation of roles and expectations. Sometimes it may seem that the effort is not worth it. However, if you do a good job of identifying good partners and working closely with them, the return on the investment should result in teen engagement and growth. Indeed, the library's best services may reach teens indirectly, the main access point being the community group with the most credibility with teen tech fringers. Let that group serve as a conduit to introduce their "clients" to the library's services.

Public Relations

High-quality programs and focused intent forms the basis for good public relations: communicating to targeted teens and relevant community members in order to gain their understanding and acceptance. Personal contact and word-of-mouth remain the more effective way to build clientele. For indeed, effective and ongoing relationships with the community are vital for success.

To this end, work to develop a coordinated PR effort. If the objective is to help teens use technology effectively, then identify their unique niche and create a compelling message that will get the audience—teens and community—to act on it. By now, that niche should be easy to state: free and supportive access to a variety of technologies that add value to teens' lives.

As mentioned in Chapter 4, your PR efforts should be strategically planned in order to optimize their impact. Thus, the tools used to deliver the message and the process by which the message is sent must be determined. Within the framework of this discussion, working with community members, the first consideration has to be the community's world and perceptions.

How does the library fit into their reality and enhance it? Usually one-shot approaches do not work, although a useful way for you to develop good public relations is to collaborate with a community entity on a short-term, concrete initiative that impacts targeted teens. Through planning and working together, both parties get to know each other better and can build a trusting relationship. A strong long-term relationship can blossom as a result of ongoing successful collaborations. In the process, your library should have a "branded" core message that can serve as a sustained reminder whenever and however communications occur. Major campaigns to publicize a specific program or effort can then build on that message, and garner strong community support.

The following case study provides concrete guidance. For instance, libraries might use the American Library Association (ALA) branding campaign, targeting it to teens: "Get Ahead @ your library" or "Power Up @ your library" or "Network @ your library" (ALA, 2003). The latter slogan could also work for the local community audience. You would need to canvas the community's teens to ascertain priority needs and interests relative to getting teens on the fringes of technology involved.

At this point, you may want to focus on one particular subgroup, for example, girls or Latinos. The library program might consist of a Latinos-only computer club where participants would learn about technology and use it for communications, research, and creating publications. Perhaps a culminating experience would be the creation of digital *fotonovelas*. Identify local community agencies—church groups, schools, markets, eating places, hair salons, local media—that could support this effort through donations, trainers, translators, communications, transportation, and so forth.

At this stage, the message might be changed to: "¿Que pasa en tu biblioteca?" or "Un mundo de posibilidades en tu biblioteca" or even "Cree los fotonovelas en tu biblioteca" (ALA, 2003). For this kind of program, target families as well as teenagers in order to garner support for Latino participation. Press releases would be distributed to the identified community groups as well as in ongoing library publications. Flyers can be posted in public places where Latinos meet, and local Web sites can also announce the program. Word of mouth should also be encouraged, orchestrated by a designated bilingual point person. In all cases, interested parties should be able to contact the library program coordinator by e-mail, telephone, or in person. As the program unfolds, public relations should continue, noting girls' successes and recognizing community support.

Advocacy

Libraries cannot guarantee that all teens can access and make effective use of technology, nor should they. Community coordination is a much more effective approach. Even communities might not have all the resources necessary to address the issues fully, but they can advocate for teens nevertheless. The American Library Association defines advocacy as "the process of turning passive support into educated action by stakeholders." In that respect, advocacy is more proactive than public relations. While most of the processes used in public relations hold for advocacy efforts, the main difference is that the library needs to know the facts *outside* of the library: teens' needs, available resources and services, gaps in addressing teens' needs. You also need to identify decision makers who can fill those gaps. Typically, your library would work in concert with community entities that support the same effort so partnerships in this instance are more interdependent. ALA has developed a series of advocacy tools, including a Spanish handbook (http://www.ala.org/pio/libraryadvocateshandbookspanish.pdf) for building an advocacy network for Spanish-speaking populations.

Whatever resources your library can use, you have an obligation to think about technologically disadvantaged teens, and act. Everyone's future depends on it.

Community Links

Community Technology Centers (http://www.ctcnet.org/) constitute an extensive federal effort to help teens access and use technology effectively. Both the Department of Housing and Urban Development (http://www.hud.gov/nnw/nnwindex.html) and the Department of Education (http://www.ed.gov/fund/grant/apply/AdultEd/CTC/index.html) focus on technology and literacy skills using technology tools. Youth Visions for Better Neighborhoods (YVBN) grants, for example, are designed to empower youth through training and engagement in local community building. Representative programs include:

- National City Public Library (CA): Community Computer Center: http://www.ci.national-city.ca.us/departments/library/library3.htm
- East Side House Development: http://www.eastsidehouse.org
- Street Level Youth Media (Chicago): http://streetlevel.iit.edu

The U.S. Department of Agriculture has addressed technology inequities through a community-based Children, Youth and Families at Risk (CYFAR) program. The agency recognized that "improving technology access and literacy must be conducted in the context of holistic programming that addresses the multiple needs of families and enhances their assets as well" (Lee & Adams, 2001, p. 1). This program builds on community partnerships to leverage technology access and use to help teens become more resilient and prepared for their futures within a networked environment. Adults and youth are trained to use telecommunications to find needed information and to communicate with community members and social agencies.

The following national organizations address the digital divide and offer ways to address related issues.

Association for Community Networking
http://www.afcn.org
Provides products and services for community networking, and connects people and organizations towards that end.

Digital Divide Network
http://www.digitaldividenetwork.org
Benton Foundation-sponsored consortium that conducts research and provides information about Digital Divide issues.

Education Development Center
http://main.edc.org
"An international, non-profit organization with 325 projects dedicated to enhancing learning, promoting health, and fostering a deeper understanding of the world."

LINCT Coalition
http://www.linct.org
"A group of socially concerned not-for-profit organizations and businesses working together to help people bridge the social, economic, educational, and digital communications divides in their communities."

National School Board Association
http://www.nsba.org/sbot/toolkit/Funding.html
Toolkit for supporting educational technology.

TechSoup.org
http://www.techsoup.org/
"The technology place for nonprofits."

Tomas Rivera Policy Institute Digital Steppingstones Initiative
http://www.trpi.org/pages/IT.html

Provides positive examples of diverse learning communities that incorporate technology.

U.S. Department of Education Digital Divide
http://www.ed.gov/Technology/digdiv.html
Assists the education community with meeting the national goals for educational technology.

Young Americans & the Digital Future
http://www.childrenspartnership.org/youngamericans/index.html
Multiyear program to promote state and local policies that increase young Americans' access to the benefits of the Internet and other information technologies.

A WORD OF CAUTION

After reading this book, you may well feel overwhelmed. There are so many teens on the digital fringes. How can you and your library address all those needs? The short answer is that no one person can do it all. Too often the librarian who serves young adults, all young adults, is seen as the one link to library services. Such an approach is sure to result in overwork and undervalued service. Youth-serving librarians cannot expect to address all the issues of teens on the fringes of technology. It takes your entire library staff and community stakeholders to influence young adults to take the technology plunge.

On the positive side, when the entire community works together to include all young adults in meaningful activities that incorporate technology, then the whole community can benefit. The library, as a center of information and instruction, can play a vital role in this vital endeavor.

WORKS CITED

American Library Association. (2003). *Library advocate's handbook.* (Spanish ed.) Chicago: American Library Association. http://www.ala.org/pio/library advocateshandbookspanish.pdf.

Bard, T. (1999). *Student assistants in the school library media center.* Englewood, CO: Teacher Ideas Press.

Braun, L. (2003). *Technically involved: Technology-based youth participation activities for your library.* Chicago: American Library Association.

Farmer, L. (1997). *Training student library staff.* Worthington, OH: Linworth.

Farmer, L. (1994). *Leadership within the school library and beyond.* Worthington, OH: Linworth.

Gambone, M., Klem, A., & Connell, J. (2002). *Finding out what matters for youth:*

Testing key links in a community action framework for youth development. Philadelphia: Youth Development Strategies.

Greene, G., & Kochhar-Bryant, C. (2003). *Pathways to successful transition for youth with disabilities.* Upper Saddle River, NJ: Merrill.

Lee, F., & Adams, N. (2001). *The digital divide: What have we done? What have we learned?* Washington, DC: CYFAR.

McCabe, R. (2001). *Civic librarianship: Renewing the social mission of the public library.* Lanham, MD: Scarecrow Press.

O'Dell, K. (2002). *Library materials and services for teen girls.* Westport, CT: Libraries Unlimited.

Technology Counts 2001. (2001, May 10). *Education Week.*

Wiles, J., & Bondi, J. (1993). *An exemplary middle school.* Upper Saddle River, NJ: Merrill-Prentice Hall.

Young Adult Library Services Association. (2003). *Young adults deserve the best: Competencies for librarians serving youth.* Chicago: American Library Association. http://www.ala.org/ala/yalsa/profdek/yacompetencies/competencies.htm.

2

TEENS IN NEED OF TECHNOLOGY

some days are way too hard for me
and i'm red with anger
boiling like a pot of water
with big popping sounds
that keeps me from feelin'
way too sorry for myself
cuz life is more tough
than i ever could imagine . . .
sometimes a pain cuts through
my heart life a knife mincing
cabbage and pieces of me
lie shredded in a pool of rage
and tears.

Jane Guttman

Before you try to "fix" or help teens, you need to know more about them. If the only deficit in adolescent lives were the absence of technology, then your job would be relatively simple. However, lack of technology exposure, let alone expertise, may be only one of many other challenges a teen faces. Teens at risk often display a cluster of problematic behaviors resulting from various factors that impact them. These same factors, and the resulting behaviors affect technological access, learning, and skill acquisition. Examining and understanding these influential factors can help you devise ways to relate to teens and support their efforts.

TODAY'S ADOLESCENTS

What makes today's teenagers special? Although some things stay the same, today's teens comprise a *new* generation: more than 75 million in number. With more than a third of them non-Anglo, these teens are more diverse than prior twentieth-century generations (Merritt, 2002). Beloit University (2003) researches contemporary culture and develops a profile of entering college freshmen for each year. The class of 2007 shares these characteristics:

- Iraq has always been a problem.
- Bert and Ernie are old enough to be their parents.
- An automatic is a weapon, not a transmission.
- There has always been a screening test for AIDS.
- Gas has always been unleaded.
- There has always been some association between fried eggs and your brain.
- Computers have always fit in their backpacks.
- They have never gotten excited over a telegram, a long distance call, or a fax.
- Test-tube babies are now having their own babies.
- Stores have always had scanners at the checkout.

According to the U.S. Department of Health and Human Services Administration of Children and Families in their 2002 study on America's youth, today's teenagers are faring better than their counterparts a decade ago.

- As of 2000, almost 40 million youth ages 10 to 19 live in the United States, roughly the same number ages 10 to 14 and 15 to 19.
- Forty-nine percent are female and 51 percent are male.
- Ninety-two percent engage in at least one positive activity that promotes well-being, and there has been a sharp decline in

health-risk behavior. For instance, only 9 percent use illicit drugs. Serious youth crime has decreased to its lowest level in two decades, and the use of firearms has also decreased.

- Students are taking more challenging school subjects, and 85 percent graduated from high school.
- About 3.3 million youths now work and nearly 80 percent have held a job at some time. About 55 percent have done volunteer work.
- More than three-quarters of American teens go to their parents for advice and consider that getting enough family time is the most important issue in their lives.

Still, youth are encountering increased incidences of crime, violence, homelessness, and substance abuse. Raffoul and McNeece (1996) note these statistics:

- A quarter of youth live in poverty and in single-parent homes (headed 97 percent of the time by women, 80 percent of whom work).
- More than 600,000 youth reside in institutions or foster care; most are either younger than 5-years-old, or are between the ages of 13 and 15. Three hundred and sixty thousand are in correctional residential facilities; five-sixths are male, and two-thirds are ethnic minorities.
- A half-million children are born each year to teenage mothers.
- One-sixth of today's youth lack access to health care.

Homicide and suicide are the leading causes of death among adolescents. Additionally, the growth in the number of adolescents will result in more job competition, just as globalization means that work may go to foreign laborers. Simultaneously, more youth are undereducated and ill prepared for the workplace. The U.S. economy remains problematic, with less support for social institutions at the same time that more accountability is being demanded. Issues of security and privacy have become problematic; youth do not feel as safe these days. Nor are other countries faring better than the United States, with racism and inequalities still rampant worldwide. No wonder that today's youth tend to be pessimistic about the future.

In the midst of these realities, today's teens have grown up in a technological environment where most are comfortable using several media simultaneously.

- Most households with children have either a computer system or video game equipment alongside a television, telephone or cell phone, and radio. The cost of equipment has generally fallen over time.
- Media have become like wallpaper in teens' lives: a ubiquitous background presence. More than 90 percent of teens use computers, and 75 percent use the Internet. (National Center for Education Statistics, 2003)
- Especially in inner cities and among minorities, adolescents use computers more at school than at home or elsewhere; however, teens are more likely to access the Internet at home than at school.
- Although teens prefer popular culture Web sites to educational ones, they spend about the same amount of time working on school assignments, accessing the Net, and playing games on computers.
- While e-consumerism has increased, so too have teen-developed Web sites reflecting personal and social issues.
- Telecommunications has become a way of life for many teens. (Center for Media Education, 2001)

In short, today's teens represent an overwhelming diversity of characteristics and experiences. Their options are greater than ever before, but with the challenges that they face, many teens are not in a position to take advantage of technology for their own development.

ADOLESCENT DEVELOPMENT

Each teenager is unique, yet all teens share certain developmental tasks to insure positive experiences in adolescence as well as a successful transition into adulthood. On the most basic level, teens need to move toward independence, deal with the future, address sexuality issues, and develop personal values and direction. The nonpartisan children's research organization, Child Trends, classifies desirable youth development outcomes into four major categories: educational achievement and cognitive attainment, health and safety, social and emotional development, and self-sufficiency. Simpson (2001) posits ten tasks for adolescents:

- get adjusted to physical bodily changes and emotions
- think abstractly
- develop a more complex perspective
- develop more rigorous decision-making and problem-solving techniques
- develop personal moral and value systems
- understand and express emotion
- develop close and supportive friendships
- develop a self-identity
- assume more responsibility
- negotiate offspring-parent relationships

To the above list James (1974) adds a number of adolescent needs that may seem diametrically opposed to each other: to be needed and to need, to belong and to be separate, to be physically active and to be still, to have intensity and risk and have routine, to get facts and imaginative stimuli.

Phelan, Davidson, and Yu (1998) examined adolescent transition in terms of "borders" that have to be negotiated:

- socio-cultural: cultural differences between family and school
- socio-economic: economic differences between family and peers
- psycho-social: emotions that distract from learning
- linguistics: communication differences between family and peers
- gender: expectation differences between boys and girls
- heterosexist: conflicts in worldview about sexuality
- structural: school environment features that impede learning, and so forth

These developmental tasks and needs represent most teenagers' realities, behaviors that are usually successfully fulfilled over time. However, the approaches that teens use to address these tasks change significantly in early, middle, and late adolescence, as noted below.

In middle school, ages 12 to 14, early teenagers are somewhat self-conscious, struggling with their own sense of identity and "normalcy." They fluctuate between a need to rely on parents and friends and seeing parents for their flaws. They often act out of emotion and may be moody. They are growing rapidly and unevenly, so they may be physically awkward, restless, and tired. Living mainly in the concrete "now," these early teenagers test adult rules and may start experimenting with risky behaviors. Girls usually are more mature than boys at this age.

In high school, ages 14 to 17, teens alternate between poor self-esteem and high self-expectations. They may seem overly critical of their own appearance and of their parents. They search actively for peer acceptance and group identity, yet feel sad about their loss of closeness with their parents. They are starting to develop career goals and are exploring their sexuality.

Older teenagers, ages 17 to 19, have a more realistic self-concept and a more stable personality. They are able to think independently and abstractly. They take pride in their own work, are able to delay gratification, and make reasonable compromises. They make serious career decisions and consider serious sexual relationships. They also accept social institutions and cultural traditions (American Academy of Child and Adolescent Psychiatry, 2003).

Obviously, attitudes and behaviors vary among individual teenagers, but the steps cross most cultures. Moreover, most teenagers manage to grow up without too much difficulty. As long as teens learn how to be productive, are able to navigate through difficulty, stay physically and mentally fit, have healthy relationships, and get involved in communities, they will succeed (Gambone, Klem, & Connell, 2002).

However, personal and societal problems can disrupt adolescent growth. In those cases, timely interventions can help mitigate obstacles. When these issues are hard to avoid, such as rural isolation or endemic poverty, then persistent problems can impact adult success if teens do not know how to cope. Symptoms of stress and difficulties include personality changes, low self-esteem, social problems, academic problems, withdrawal, and avoidance (Williams-Boyd, 2003).

The term resiliency refers to a person's ability to adapt and transform in the face of adversity, to bounce back (Benard, 1995). Traditionally, resilience has been subdivided into four elements of well-being: physical, emotional, mental, and spiritual (HeavyRunner & Morris, 1997). These qualities are particularly necessary for teens. The Search Institute in Minneapolis (http://www.search-institute.org) has developed a list of forty internal and external qualities that help teens through troubled times; these are called developmental assets. When teens use these assets, they are more likely to succeed and be more resilient. Specifically,

- family support and love that is communicated, parents who are involved in the teenager's education and expect academic success, familial supervision and monitoring, positive parental role models

- adults outside the family (at least three teachers, librarians, coaches, youth leaders, and so on) who provide positive modeling and support
- neighbors who care, monitor, and value youth
- communities where teens have a positive role and responsibility, community organizations and religious institutions that engage teens weekly in service and creative activities
- schools that give encouragement and care, administrators who communicate clear boundaries and expectations, creative opportunities
- friends who model positive behavior
- environment of safety

In particular, teens who lack resiliency often seem disconnected. As teens grow up, about a third of them feel disconnected from institutions (e.g., school) or people (e.g., peers, families, community) for at least six months, with at least 50 percent of Latino and African American males exhibiting these signs (Besharov, 1999). Ethnicity in itself has no significant effect on how teens respond to these factors. Teens most at risk for disconnectedness include those who have parents who dropped out of school, families on welfare, one or no parents available, low intellect, academic failure, children of their own, or drug-abuse problems.

Interestingly, few young adults feel disconnected before their junior year in high school; the typical tasks of older teens—seeking work, making sexual decisions, considering military options—seem to constitute a psychological bridge that some teens fear crossing. Short-term disconnected youth generally do not suffer social or financial problems—especially if they have personal characteristics and family support systems that can overcome obstacles—and go on to be successful adults. However, youth who feel disconnected for three or more years suffer long-term social and financial problems (Besharov, 1999).

In identifying technologically deficient teens, one notices that such individuals typically lack those assets of external support, empowerment, expectations, and use of time. They are disconnected not only from technology, but from other aspects of life. To make the situation more serious, studies show that at-risk behaviors tend to cluster so that teenagers display multiple symptoms of dysfunctional behaviors (Chatman, 1996).

UNDERSERVED GROUPS

Generally, teens on the technology fringe are also on the educational and societal fringes. Why? Many have difficulties from the start: health-risk factors dating to before they were born, economic factors that impact them and their community, cultural factors such as values and language that differ from the dominant school culture, and physical differences. Others have situational stress due to sexual activity, violent behavior, accidents, family unemployment, and so forth.

At-risk teens usually do not have the safety net that over a substantial period of time help them successfully resolve "outside" crises. To further explain this situation, one can use the analogy of being "broke" to being poor: the former is short-term, the latter is a substantive condition.

Chatman's 1996 research on the characteristics of the information poor reinforces the issues of the technology poor. She notes that these individuals:

- do not think they can help themselves
- behave secretly and deceptively in order to protect what information they have
- do not take social risks
- do not think that those people outside their class would share information with them
- do not think much outside information is relevant to them
- exhibit "self-protective behaviors . . . in response to social norms" (e.g., if peers or school devalue a teen, that teen will defend himself) (pp. 197–198)

It should be noted that these "tech-nots" may well be successful within their own subculture—be it ethnicity, gender, geography, or values. That is, they have social capital within their sphere of influence. Too often, those in political and economic power perceive the Other as innately deficient and lacking desirable personal qualities. So while certain teenagers may lack technological skills, they may not see that as a problem within their own cultural norms.

The critical issue is that teens, like all people, must feel comfortable in their primary social environment in order to survive, and they also need to form bonds with other cultures, particularly the dominant one, in order to succeed in the public arena. Technology can be an effective means to empower teens within their favored culture as well as provide a means to connect with other cultures, particularly those with socioeconomic power. By effectively using technology, teens can improve themselves *and* can work with others to reach their goals (Keeble & Loader, 2001).

Poor

Probably the most well-known and largest groups of teens who do not have adequate access or training in technology are the poor. Who are they?

- Forty percent are minors, although they constitute 25 percent of the total population.
- The majority live in inner cities.
- Almost 60 percent of Blacks and 70 percent of Latinos live in large urban areas and are likely to live in high-poverty areas.
- The poorest families are headed by single mothers; almost 40 percent of Black families fit that profile. In contrast, only 8.6 percent of non-Latino whites are poor.
- Education is also an indicator of income, although Blacks earn less than whites, and women earn less than men, with the same education.

Severely distressed neighborhoods exhibit the following elements:

- High poverty rate, female head of household, high male unemployment rate, and a high school-dropout rate.
- The number of children in these neighborhoods rose from 4.7 to 5.7 million from 1990 to 2000; 55 percent are Black, and 29 percent are Latino.
- Twenty-eight percent of Black children live in distressed neighborhoods, 13 percent of Latino children, and 1 percent of Anglo children. Neighborhoods determine day care options, job options, and degree of safety.

With poverty comes greater risks for other problems. Poorer housing, inappropriate sanitation, and limited cooking facilities lead to malnutrition and health problems. Inner-city poor and minorities tend to abuse substances more than the overall U.S. population. Such abuse can lead to health problems, violence, and high-risk sexual behavior. In fact, violence leads to the single largest health problem among Black male teenagers. Poor women have a higher risk of getting infected with HIV because of greater exposure to rape and to multiple sexual partners, as well as increased drug use. The main social risk factors associated with poverty are violence, low educational achievement, and eventual unemployment. Psychologically, the poor are more prone to stress, anxiety, and depression because of limited choices in terms of satisfying the basic needs of safety and shelter (Zuvekas, 1999).

Technology is seldom a high priority among the poor, who are scrounging for shelter, food, and clothing. Particularly as the poor are more likely to move from one place to another, they lack the stability to own computers and subscribe to ISPs to provide ongoing services. One bright light in this picture is the advent of cellular phones. These devices are often the most stable form of communication for the poor because of their portability. As cell phone models become more sophisticated and cost-effective, the poor will have a greater chance of getting Internet access, so they can access information as needed.

Homeless

Two million Americans are in homeless situations each year. Among homeless families, 84 percent are headed by females, 43 percent are African American, and 38 percent are Anglos (National Association of Counties, 1999). At its very core, homelessness is a precarious situation in terms of health and social risks.

The search for food and clothing sometimes leads to involvement in the sex trade. Many homeless youth have a history of sex abuse. In a study of homeless youth in Los Angeles, 71 percent had a substance abuse disorder. At Covenant House (a large Catholic child care agency providing shelter and services to homeless and runaway youth), 80 percent had a substance abuse history. Homeless youth are exposed to more violence and often dealt with it before they lost their homes (Zuvekas, 1999). As noted above, cellular phones can serve as a stable connection to the outside world when home addresses cannot.

Teens of Color

Even in the twenty-first century, race and ethnicity impact scholastic achievement and social status. The Educational Testing Service asserted that "educational inequalities begin at birth" (Viadero, 2003, p. 1) because of lower birth weight and other health factors. Blacks and Latinos are less likely to be read to by their parent(s), and are more apt to learn in overcrowded classrooms from inexperienced teachers. Additionally, they are more likely to move and change schools, which means that they have to renegotiate social relationships. Native American teens are often separated from their families and tribes as they go to distant schools for high school education. As youth get older, disparities in academic success increase so that minority teens experience greater difficulty keeping up with their Anglo peers. This lack of stability impacts educational opportunities, including the smaller probability that these teens can have regular and sustained experiences with technology. Ironically, technology has the potential to help these young people compensate for shifting family situations.

African Americans/Blacks

African American, or Black, families cover a broad spectrum of expectations and experiences. The Black community as a whole has a strong sense of social relationships and personal distinctiveness. They tend to respond to issues holistically and use internal cues to solve problems. They appreciate novelty and freedom, and have a keen sense of justice. The community also expects schools to provide their children with a good education (Josey & DeLoach, 2000). Still, African Americans are overrepresented among the urban poor where the economic gap is widening. Overcrowding and crime impact family life and teen development.

Black teenagers, as a rule, use language expressively and complement speech with nuanced body language. They place a high value on personal relationships, sometimes to the detriment of academic achievement. Part of teen development involves taking risks, but in dangerous neighborhoods such behavior can have serious consequences. Murder is the number one cause of death among African American youth and teen suicide tripled between 1960 and 1988 (Levine & Rosich, 1996). With societal prejudice against Black teenage males in particular, these young men have a harder time getting jobs and sustaining strong families. Tatum (2003) asserts that Black males need a safe environment in which to search for meaning in their lives and the means to challenge the status quo, analyze society, and improve it.

Technology can provide a means to empower African American youth; access to online information is an "alternative to conventional teacher-directed on-site paradigm; informational justice is a human rights issue" (Josey & DeLoach, 2000, p. 601). In an editorial in *Black Enterprise* (March, 1998), Muhammad asserted that Blacks have opportunities to access the Internet: "The only thing holding us back is our own foresight."

Economically secure African Americans own computers and use technology at work and at home to the same extent as other ethnicities. Still, poor Blacks have fewer computers than poor whites. Several reasons may account for this difference: less community-based investment or public funding for connectivity infrastructure, lack of knowledge about technology and its benefits, little Internet content that address their needs, distrust of government and big business interaction with technology.

Latinos

Latinos comprise a variety of subgroups, from Californian land grant descendants to recent Haitian refugees. Two-thirds were born in the United States, and three-quarters speak Spanish at home. Latinos constitute the fastest growing ethnicity in the United States, and are younger than the general population. Most Latinos speak Spanish and develop self-esteem from being part of the family. They tend to have less education, and a quarter of them live in poverty. Puerto Rican families have a high rate of divorce and female heads-of-households, about the same as African Americans. This situation is the result of overcrowded urban living conditions, the need for women to work, and adjustments in immigrating (Rice, 1998, p. 70).

Almost 75 percent of Mexican Americans live a segregated life in urban barrios. Many Mexican American children do not start school with the same advantages as other students for several reasons: less exposure to rich cognitive experiences, parental lack of much formal schooling and might not speak English at home, and free and open conversation that might be discouraged in authoritarian environments. In school, teachers might not be able to speak Spanish, and they may react negatively to Spanish being spoken by students (Rice, 1998).

Adolescence can be even more stressful for Mexican Americans. These teens are particularly worried about issues that affect the family: illness, crime, alcohol abuse, moving, unemployment. Additionally, the tight family structure can discourage independence, especially for girls. Oldest sons are sometimes indulged and given greater freedom, but not expected to achieve academically. Risk taking is not encouraged; rather, youth are told to be careful and not shame the family, so as a result they may be less competitive than their Anglo peers. Latino tends tend to get married earlier than other ethnicities, drop out of school earlier, and get lower-paying jobs (Moller, 2001).

Latinos have lower computer ownership, have less access to the Internet, and use computers to a lesser extent than any other ethnic group in the United States because of possible economic limitations, less education, and non-citizen status (Luevano-Molina, 2001, p. 134).

Native Americans

Native Americans have the highest birth rate, highest death rate, and shortest life expectancy of any ethnic group in the United States. They have one of the highest unemployment rates, lowest income levels, and overall low standards of living. Furthermore, they suffer from hunger and malnutrition more than other ethnic group (Rice, 1998, p. 72). Their leading illness is middle ear disease, resulting in hearing loss, which impacts academic skills (Rice, 1998, p. 73).

Native and Alaska Indian teenagers have to manage the often-conflicting cultures of Anglo educational expectations and family values. Many feel despair, and the suicide rate among this teenage population is two and one-half-times higher than the combined rate of all the other ethnicities. In fact, the leading causes of death among this population are accidents, suicides, and homicides (Hernandez, 2002). In contrast, resilient youth tend to think of themselves as bicultural, taking the positive aspects of each environment (Strand & Peacock, 2002). In terms of technology, Native and Alaska Indian homelands are often isolated, which impedes Internet connectivity.

Other at-risk factors for Native- and Alaskan-Indian teenagers focus on family situations: single-mother households where the mother had children before she was 20-years-old, high unemployment, teens sent to boarding schools that separate them from their communities, and family alienation from mainstream institutions (Clarke, 2002).

Clarke's 2002 meta-analysis of research on risk factors among this population revealed other startling statistics:

- illicit drug use was more than twice as high (22.2 percent) as the national average (9.7 percent);

- binge alcohol use was higher (13.8 percent) than the national average (10.3 percent);
- heavy alcohol use was higher (3.8 percent) than the national average (2.5 percent);
- use of cigarettes was more than twice as high (27.2 percent) as the national average (13.4 percent); and
- taking part in at least one group-against-group fight in the past year was higher (22.4 percent) than the national average (16.1 percent) (2002).

While there are no recent data about Native and Alaskan Indian drop-out rates, national studies from a decade ago indicated that Native American student drop-out rates were higher than other groups in the United States (Hillabrant, Romano, Stang, & Charleston, 1991). It is important to look beyond the youth themselves and examine conditions in the schools they attend. Bowker's 2003 study of Native American women reported that female students who dropped out cited several school-related problems: failure or inability to get along with teachers, dislike of school, inability to get along with other students, boredom, feelings of not belonging, and suspension from school.

According to Caine and Caine (1997), students who are confronted with racist threats on a regular basis often lose a positive sense of cultural identity and begin a process of downshifting, which eventually leads to dropping out. Similarly, Irvine (1990) suggests that when there is a cultural incongruity between the school and the student, miscommunication and confrontation often occur among students, teachers, and families, resulting in hostility, alienation, and eventual dropping out (Clarke, 2002). Technology, which has traditionally been associated with Anglo education, may be summarily rejected in the process, even though Native and Alaskan Indian communities are starting to use these tools to preserve and share their culture.

Immigrants

In the United States there are 32 million immigrants, about a tenth of the population, mainly due to globalization, poverty, and political unrest. About half are women. Because of mass media, recent immigrants tend to be more knowledgeable about the United States than prior generations. Yet the dominant culture in the United States generally displays a xenophobic attitude, even though almost everyone's family immigrated to the United States at one time. As a result, conflicts with immigrants arise in terms of race, language, jobs, and communication between different generations (Luevano-Molina, 2001).

The foreign-born are more likely to be poor. About a fifth of the foreign-born without a U.S. citizen parent live below the poverty line, and a quarter of noncitizens are poor as compared to 11.4 percent of naturalized citizens (Zuvekas, 1999, p. 3). Moreover, culture shock can lead to depression and a sense of isolation. Immigrants between the ages of 12 and 24 are particularly vulnerable to attempting suicide (Zuvekas, 1999). Those immigrants who cannot speak English have less access to health and other social services. In some non-U.S. cultures, health issues are not discussed, and preventive medical treatment or Western medicine is not pursued. It should be noted that English language learner (ELL) immigrants are more likely to want Internet information in their primary language than those who were born in the United States.

Acculturation is particularly difficult for immigrant teens because they want to feel like they belong, but are torn between two or more cultures. Their peers may consider them foreigners and outsiders; their own parents may think that they are abandoning family values. Not only does each ethnic group have its own identity, but those immigrants who came as refugees have an additional identity to confront and may have to overcome tragic experiences. It should also be noted that refugee teens may well be more educated and sophisticated than their parents, which upsets the traditional authority of elders and reverses the roles of responsibility.

As immigrants deal with at least two significant cultures, their own and the dominant Anglo, they make decisions about how to balance their allegiances.

- They may stay with their primary culture and withdraw from the dominant one; they may choose to remain social outsiders.
- They may reject their original culture and embrace wholeheartedly the Anglo dominant culture, and thus become over acculturated. Family stress may well rise as a result.
- They may assume most of the values of the dominant culture and maintain the trappings of their original culture, thus becoming mainstream. They may reject both cultures and become marginalized.

- They may accept both cultures, drawing strengths from each and thus become bicultural (HeavyRunner & Morris, 1997).

Educational and library experiences can be problematic for immigrant teens because of first-country differences in practices and values. In many developing countries library service is not free; patrons have to rent books. Additionally, in some countries (such as Cambodia) records are kept and used to harm the intelligencia in times of revolution. Not only may immigrants lack knowledge about these institutions and their benefits, but they may also harbor negative attitudes toward government. Coupled with the fact that immigrants may not be members of mainstream social groups is the problem of language barriers and lack of understanding about library use in the United States. Teens, in particular, may link the library with homework, not with personal or recreational needs. Literacy efforts may also suffer, not only because of language differences, but also because U.S. education tends to favor English-only instruction. Moreover, in some countries, reading is not considered very important. With immigrant families focusing on survival and acculturation, education and technology usually take a backseat (Constantino, 1998). On the face of it, learning how to "surf the Net" may seem frivolous as well as costly, but the Internet can be accessed free in libraries, and online content can provide timely social agency help, for instance, that could then open up doors for longer-term goals.

English Language Learners

English language learners (ELL) may be subdivided into two categories: those born abroad and those born in the United States. In both cases, there are many roadblocks to informational, technological, and textual literacy: sociopolitical differences, economic conditions, xenophobia, antibilingual education, prejudicial institutional culture, lack of teacher knowledge about ELL, orthographical differences, and different cultural values relative to reading (Grant & Wong, 2003).

If they are out of the social loop, ELL teens are less likely to have experienced technology and so are unlikely to see its benefits. Even if they used technology in their first country, it may seem hard to find or costly to access in their new country, resulting in lower ELL usage. On the one hand, for ELL readers of non-Roman language systems, English-only software and Internet browsers can be particularly daunting. On the other hand, however, when teens find out about online translation programs and readable documents in their original language, they can bridge their primary culture to that of the United States, using a variety of contextual cues.

Migrant Farmworkers

Migrant workers often face the same obstacles as the traditional poor and immigrant populations. There are more workers than housing units, so issues of homelessness also apply to them. They are exposed to pesticides and other unhealthy living conditions. Additionally, because they move often, migrant workers seldom have consistent health care or education (Zuvekas, 1999). It should be noted that 81 percent of migrant farmworkers are foreign-born, and only 22 percent are U.S. citizens. Yet they constitute 64 percent of the harvest labor force (Huang, 2002).

Not only are these teens transient, but 85 percent of the youth respondents in a 2001 Harvard study sample were separated from one or both parents during the process of migration. Significant differences between the ethnic groups exist. Children of Chinese heritage tended to migrate with both parents most frequently (37 percent). In contrast, the circumstances of migration for the Haitian and Central American groups imposed a family disruption during migration for 96 percent of them.

Nearly half (49 percent) of youth respondents in the sample were separated from both parents sometime during migration. Separation from both parents was most likely to occur among the Central American (80 percent), Dominican (61 percent), and Haitian (59 percent) families (Harvard Graduate School of Education, 2003).

Because of their transient status, it may be hard for you to even find out about these youth, let alone get them into the library. There are several sources of information you can access that can help in this process: Department of Agriculture (http://www.usda.gov), Department of Labor (http://www.dol.gov), Cooperative Extension Program (http://www.reeusda.gov), and other regulatory agencies. Migrant program administrators and recruiters can also be good contacts (Melecio & Hanley, 2002).

Teens need a sense of stability, and maintaining a steady human network can facilitate access to technology. With the presence of the Internet with its worldwide resources and mobile communications properties, today's migrant teens can actually keep connected with educational and library systems better than before. In order to take advantage of technology, however, they must become aware of what options are available. The key to success is a good infrastructure that is established systematically for all migrant youth, with support from their families.

Rural and Isolated Populations

About 16 percent of the rural population lives in poverty (Zuvekas, 1999, p. 1). Educational opportunities traditionally have been limited because of low-income communities and poor access to a variety of resources. These factors also impact the quality of education when school personnel leave out of frustration, resulting in revolving-door employment (Howley & Pendarvis, 2002).

On the other hand, small schools can facilitate a strong sense of community, which can help teens feel socially and emotionally connected. These environments call for and facilitate cross-agency collaboration in order to build capacity to provide effective services.

As with Native Americans, rural teens can benefit from technology because it offsets isolation and provides access to resources worldwide and subject matter educational specialists. Rural teens can develop social cyber-connections with teens from other settings. The two main obstacles to this kind of activity are economic (paying for equipment and connectivity) and geographic (establishing telecommunications lines). Wireless solutions are beginning to help ameliorate the problem, but too many areas are still without connectivity.

Gang Members

Usually youth who are involved in gangs live in poverty, have family stress, and drop out of school. They experience school failure and a sense of alienation. Moreover, the majority of incarcerated gang members have some kind of learning disability (Eisenman, 1993). With few employment skills and limited opportunities for conventional success, few gang members have any hope for the future. Not surprisingly, most are involved in violent behavior, drug abuse, and criminal action.

Minorities tend to be overrepresented in gangs. As they lose their connections to traditional cultural ways and confront urban realities, for instance Native Americans, and particularly younger teens, are becoming increasingly involved in gang behavior Clarke (2002). Recent immigrant teens may also find themselves involved in gang-related behavior as a way to fend for themselves in an alien and sometimes hostile environment (Hernandez, 2002).

While gangs increasingly use the Internet to recruit members or discuss crime methods, most teenage gang members are less likely than their non-gang peers to use technology (National Alliance of Gang Investigators Associations, 2004). Coming from poor families and neighborhoods, they have less access to equipment and Internet connectivity. Often experiencing failure in school and more likely to be truant, they have fewer opportunities to learn how to use technology. Additionally, since many youth who join gangs do so out of a need to belong, the probability that they feel connected to "techies" is low (Flannery & Huff, 1999). On the other hand, when at-risk teens are given opportunities to learn how to use technology to improve their surroundings while earning money and developing peer relationships, they are less likely to join gangs (United Teen Equity Center, 2004).

Incarcerated Youth

In the United States, some 2,000 children and adolescents are imprisoned in adult facilities daily (Eisenmann, 1993). Older adolescents, ages 15 to 17, are most likely to be incarcerated, and are typically repeat offenders. Their crimes usually consist of property-related offenses or drug-related incidences. The "classic" profile of an adolescent most at risk to become incarcerated is a poor, illiterate, low school performing, aggressive Black male gang member from a dysfunctional family. Non-Anglos constitute the vast majority in the penal system, and low academic achievement is the norm; more than 70 percent of incarcerated youth have learning disabilities. Not only do they tend to have little family support, they were usually abused by relatives. In addition, most incarcerated youth have health problems. Furthermore, illiterate and English language learners are at a distinct disadvantage in being able to take advantage of any technology that might be available.

School Dropouts

Urban centers tend to overrepresent teen dropouts. For instance, in a 1991 study of Chicago schools, there was an overall dropout rate of 53 percent, with Black and Latino areas showing 65 percent dropout rates. Even in 2000, the dropout rate for Latinos was 56 percent (Leonardo, 2003). The highest dropout rate, however, was for Latinas because of cultural values.

Dropouts often have had negative experiences at school. They might be struggling readers, or they might have encountered social prejudice. They are usually not engaged in the school environment, and may feel alienated, thinking no one cares for them.

In other cases, family or neighborhood stresses may lead to dropping out. Typical situations include the need to take care of family members, earn money to support the family, or protect the family from unsafe surroundings. Peer, family, and cultural norms may also conflict with school expectations, and teens may find themselves rejecting school for other options in life (Bowker, 2003).

Because many dropouts come from impoverished or unstable families, their major access to technology is through schools, so they are unlikely to get the technology skills that they need. Also, since they associate technology with their negative school experience, they are not inclined to make an effort to become information literate.

Teenage Parents

Although the majority of high schoolers abstain from sexual intercourse, and the birth rate for girls ages 15 to 17 is at a record low (30 births per 1,000 girls), the percentage of adolescent parents is higher than for other developed nations, and the abortion rate is lower. Moreover, most U.S. teenage mothers tend to choose to keep their children rather than give them up for adoption (Lerner & Lerner, 2001).

Early parenthood impacts teenage development socially and emotionally. They tend to leave school earlier, have lower-paying jobs or be unemployed, have fewer material and social resources, have subsequent pregnancies, have more difficulty with family relations, and have less stability in their lives. (It should be noted that outcomes for low-income teenage mothers often do not differ from their nonparent peers because the negative effects of poverty overpower other considerations.)

Issues surrounding teenage pregnancy and parenthood differ for young and older teens. Younger girls are at a different point in their developmental tasks (e.g., menarche, peer affiliation, cognition, moral development), so interference in those tasks can result in more difficulties in adulthood. Furthermore, they—and their offspring—tend to have more medical complications associated with their pregnancies. In both cases however, not only is their own adolescent development impacted, but teen parents also have to help their children develop in positive ways.

In brief, because of the high demands of teenage parenthood, and the diminished resources usually associated with this population, technology is often not a high priority in their lives. Still, having access to parenting information, being able to communicate with parenting experts—as well as other teenage parents—for support, and learning technology skills to facilitate work entry, would help these young parents succeed.

Girls

While not usually lumped categorically with the homeless and isolated, teenage girls constitute a fringe group relative to technology. Although females make up the majority of telecommunications users, they do not represent an equal proportion of technology career employees. Girls are not so much intimidated by technology as much as they are uninterested in getting involved in the stereotypical technology culture, that of smelly nerds playing violent video games. Girls are surprisingly unaware of technology career options and frequently are not counseled to take the appropriate prerequisite courses so they can be prepared at the college level. When girls *do* take the mainstay programming courses, they are usually far outnumbered by boys, and the assignments tend to be math and science oriented (American Association of University Women, 2000).

There are three reasons that part of the blame for this disenfranchisement lies with parents and educators: (1) They hold old stereotypical views of technology careers; (2) they have old stereotypical views of career options for females; and (3) they know little about technology themselves. Occasionally, they assume that *all* teenagers—boys and girls—know all about technology so they do not give technology career information proactively.

Parents, for their part, are more likely to buy systems for their sons than for their daughters. At school, boys may monopolize the computers so girls do not have the same opportunities to explore and practice. Thus, school and community members must provide conscious interventions to insure equitable physical and intellectual access to technology and the opportunities surrounding them.

The Disabled

At any point in time, about 20 percent of the U.S. population is disabled. Indeed, it can be said that everyone becomes disabled at some point in life because of accidents or aging. Nevertheless, the present and future of teens with disabilities can be daunting. Because of the higher demands on their families, the divorce rate is higher than for families without disabled children. Over a quarter of disabled youth drop out of school, and between one half and three-quarters become unemployed. They are less likely to form long-lasting relationships or get married. The good news is that the number of high school graduates among the disabled is growing, 80 percent want to work, and most do not need special accommodations in order to work effectively (Greene & Kochhar-Bryant, 2003, p. 9).

Teenagers with disabilities are teens first; they need to become more independent and want to develop rewarding friendships. Yet they may feel isolated and frustrated because of possible stigmas and the extra effort they may have to make. Their reasons for dropping out of school mirror those of nondisabled teens: academic failure, lack of engagement or support, drug abuse, low socioeconomic status, language barriers, or family status (single parent, low education attainment, sibling dropouts) (Greene & Kochhar-Bryant, 2003, p. 213).

Technology has a great deal to offer disabled teens. It can reduce isolation, as it does with rural and transient populations, and sophisticated technologies can actually help teens overcome disabilities. Unfortunately, however, a significant gap exists between the able and disabled: 56.7 percent access to computers and 42.1 percent Internet connectivity among the abled, compared to 28.4 percent access to computers and 21.6 percent Internet connectivity among the disabled. Likewise, 75 percent of able-bodied teens have used a computer versus 40 percent of teens with disabilities. The situation for adolescents with disabilities is even more discouraging if they are minorities or come from impoverished families (Warschauer, 2003).

IMPLICATIONS FOR LIBRARIES

This generation of adolescents represents a very mixed picture. They are certainly the most diverse group of teenagers in U.S. history, not only in terms of socioeconomics, but also in terms of their experiences. While most grow up to be productive adults, the developmental tasks that teens must resolve are sometimes harder than ever because of the societies in which they live and the options, both good and bad, that are offered to them.

The technology gene is not implanted in their brains, and not everyone has the opportunity to explore technology, in fact, a significant portion have no wish to deal with technology. Some teens are extraordinarily sophisticated in their technology use, but even they might not have a solid moral compass to help them channel their energies. The picture is not rosy.

In any case, all librarians, not just youth-serving professionals, need to understand adolescent development and the worlds in which they live. The tasks of growth are universal, but the strategies and options for teens can vary tremendously. By being aware of these differences, you can make meaningful connections with individual teens and optimize their experiences with technology.

To better understand the teens in your community, try some of these beginning steps:

- go where teens congregate: shopping malls, skate parks, recreation centers, and so on
- go to the movies and watch a teen flick
- attend an anime conference
- visit a game arcade
- read teen blogs (Web logs) and e-zines
- listen to radio stations that teens like
- get the local student newspaper
- ask for a copy of the school's yearbook
- get on mailing lists of schools and youth-serving agencies
- attend school and community events and meetings
- visit a youth group meeting: Boys and Girls Club, 4H, Girl Scouts, Catholic Youth Organization, and so on
- check out Web sites about adolescents and teen issues
- talk with parents of teenagers
- listen to teens

Many technologically disadvantaged teenagers, by their very behavior, may well slip under the social radar of these typical teen venues. In some cases, community organizations and agencies such as correctional institutions, public health, and social services agencies can serve as sources of information about the teens they encounter and serve. Youth shelters, missing children hotlines, family planning centers, churches, and crisis intervention agencies may be able to offer you insights on these youngsters' lives.

In addition, information about the parents may give some indication of their teen offspring's environment, as evidenced in census figures, welfare rolls, immigration services, and criminal records.

Work in concert with other youth-serving agencies in order to "profile" the teens in your community and try to reach them. By knowing where teens are and where they want to be, both physically and psychologically, you can begin to identify the motivating factors that will attract teens to library services and technology.

Remember that, to begin with, these teens may well have little interest in the library per se, which is another reason why working with community organizations makes sense. Technology-related library services can often be distributed through social services agencies.

Your first goal is to offer benefits in a safe, dependable environment; the finer points of library service can then follow.

WORKS CITED

Administration of Children & Families. (2002). *Profile of America's youth.* Washington, DC: U.S. Department of Health and Human Services. http://www.acf.hhs.gov/programs/fysb/youthinfo/profile.htm.

American Academy of Child and Adolescent Psychiatry. (2003). *Facts for families.* Washington, DC: American Academy of Child and Adolescent Psychiatry. http://www.aacap.org.

American Association of University Women. (2000). *Tech-savvy: Educating girls in the new computer age.* Washington, DC: AAUW.

Beloit College. (2003). *Beloit College mindset list.* Beloit, WI: Beloit College. http://www.beloit.edu/~pubaff/releases/2003/03mindsetlist.html.

Benard, B. (1995). *Fostering resilience in children.* ERIC Digest. Champaign, IL: ERIC Clearinghouse for Elementary and Early Childhood Education. (ERIC Document Reproduction Service No. ED386327).

Besharov, D. (Ed.). (1999). *America's disconnected youth.* Washington, DC: CWLA Press.

Bowker, A. (2003). *Sisters in the blood: The education of women in Native America.* Washington, DC: Office of Educational Research and Improvement.

Caine, R., & Caine, G. (1997). *Education on the edge of possibility.* Alexandria, VA: Association for Supervision and Curriculum Development.

Center for Media Education. (2001). *Teensites.com: A field guide to the new digital landscape.* Washington, DC: Center for Media Education.

Chatman, E. (1996). The impoverished lifeworld of outsiders. *Journal of the American Society for Information Science, 47,* 193–206.

Clarke, A. (2002). *Social and emotional distress among American Indian and Alaska Native students: Research findings.* ERIC Digest. Charleston, WV: ERIC Clearinghouse on Rural Education and Small Schools. (ERIC Document Reproduction Service No. EDO-RC-01-11).

Constantino, R. (Ed.). (1998). *Literacy, access, and libraries among the language minority population.* Lanham, MD: Scarecrow Press.

Eisenman, R. (1993). Characteristics of adolescent felons in a prison treatment program. *Adolescence, 28*(111), 695–699.

Flannery, D., & Huff, C. (Eds.). (1999). *Youth violence: Prevention, intervention, and social policy.* Washington, DC: American Psychiatric Press.

Gambone, M., Klem, A., & Connell, J. (2002). *Finding out what matters for youth: Testing key links in a community action framework for youth development.* Philadelphia: Youth Development Strategies.

Grant, R., & Wong, S. (2003, February). Barriers to literacy for language-minority learners: An argument for change in the literacy education profession. *Journal of Adolescent & Adult Literacy, 46*(5), 386–393.

Greene, G., & Kochhar-Bryant, C. (2003). *Pathways to successful transition for youth with disabilities.* Upper Saddle River, NJ: Merrill.

Harvard Graduate School of Education. (2003). *85 percent of immigrant children experience separations during migration.* Cambridge, MA: Harvard University. http://gseweb.harvard.edu/news/features/suarez06292001.html.

HeavyRunner, I., & Morris, J. (1997). Traditional native culture and resilience. *Research Practice, 5*(1).

Hernandez, A. (2002, December). *Can education play a role in the prevention of youth gangs in Indian country? One tribe's approach.* ERIC Digest. Charleston, WV: ERIC Clearinghouse on Rural Education and Small Schools. (ERIC Document Reproduction Service No. EDO-RC-02-12).

Hillabrant, W., Romano, M., Stang, D., & Charleston, G. M. (1991). *Native American education at a turning point: Current demographics and trends.* Washington, DC: U.S. Department of Education. Indian Nations at Risk Task Force. (ERIC Document Reproduction Service No. ED343756).

Howley, A., & Pendarvis, E. (2002, December). *Recruiting and retaining rural school administrators.* ERIC Digest. Charleston, WV: ERIC Clearinghouse on Rural Education and Small Schools. (ERIC Document Reproduction Service No. EDO-RC-02-7).

Huang, G. (2002, December). What federal statistics reveal about migrant farmworkers: A summary for education. ERIC Digest. Charleston, WV: ERIC Clearinghouse on Rural Education and Small Schools. (ERIC Document Reproduction Service No. EDO-RD-02-9).

Irvine, J. (1990). *Black students and school failure: Policies, practices, and prescriptions.* Westport, CT: Greenwood.

James, C. (1974). *Beyond custom.* New York: Agathon Press.

Josey, E., & DeLoach, M. (Eds.). (2000). *Handbook of Black librarianship.* Lanham, MD: Scarecrow.

Keeble, L., & Loader, B. (2001). *Social capital and cyberpower.* London: Routledge.

Leonardo, Z. (2003). *Ideology, discourse, and school reform.* Westport, CT: Praeger.

Lerner, J., & Lerner, R. (Eds.). (2001). *Adolescence in America: An encyclopedia.* Santa Barbara, CA: ABC-CLIO.

Levine, F., & Rosich, K. (1996). *Social causes of violence: Crafting a science agenda.* Washington, DC: American Sociological Association.

Luevano-Molina, S. (Ed.). (2001). *Immigrant politics and the public library.* Westport, CT: Greenwood.

Melecio, R., & Hanley, T. (2002, December). *Identification and recruitment of migrant students: Strategies and resources.* ERIC Digest. Charleston, WV: ERIC Clearinghouse on Rural Education and Small Schools. (ERIC Reproduction Service No. EDO-RC-02-10).

Merritt, S. (2002). The millennials: A perspective on America's next generation and their impact on higher education. PACAC Annual Conference, Seven Springs, PA, July 1.

Moller, S. (2001). *Library service to Spanish speaking patrons: A practical guide.* Englewood, CO: Libraries Unlimited.

Muhammad, T. (1998, March). About this issue. *Black Enterprise,* 13.

National Association of Counties. (1999). *The face of homelessness.* Washington, DC: National Association of Counties.

National Center for Education Statistics. (2003). *Computer and Internet use by children and adolescents in 2001.* Washington, DC: U.S. Department of Education.

The national gang threat. (2004). Sacramento, CA: National Alliance of Gang Investigations Associations. http://www.nagia.org/NGTASection_II.htm.

Phelan, P., Davidson, A., & Yu, H. (1998). *Adolescents' worlds: Negotiating family, peers, and school.* New York: Teachers College Press.

Raffoul, P., & McNeece, C. (Eds.). (1996). *Future issues of social work practice.* Boston: Allyn & Bacon.

Rice, F. (1998). *The adolescent: Development, relationships, and culture.* (9th ed.). Boston: Allyn & Bacon.

Simpson, R. (2001). *Raising teens: A synthesis of research and a foundation for action.* Boston: Harvard Center for Health Communication.

Strand, J., & Peacock, T. (2002, December). *Nurturing resilience and school success for American Indian and Alaska native students.* ERIC Digest. Charleston, WV: ERIC Clearinghouse on Rural Education and Small Schools. (ERIC Document Reproduction Service No. EDO-RC-02-11).

Tatum, A. (2003, May). All degreed and nowhere to go: Black males and literacy education. *Journal of Adolescent & Adult Literacy, 46*(8), 620–623.

United Teen Equality Center. (2004). Lowell, MA: United Teen Equality Center. http://www.utec-lowell.org/index.php.

Viadero, E. (2003, November 26). Study probes factors fueling achievement gaps. *Education Week, 23*(13), 1, 12.

Warschauer, M. (2003). *Technology and social inclusion: Rethinking the digital divide.* Cambridge, MA: MIT Press.

Williams-Boyd, P. (Ed.). (2003). *Middle grades education.* Santa Barbara, CA: ABC-CLIO.

Zuvekas, A., et al. (1999). *Mini environment assessment of the health status and needs of the poor.* Washington, DC: George Washington University. http://www.gwhealthpolicy.org/downloads/ascension99.pdf.

3

TECHNOLOGY AND LIFE AFTER HIGH SCHOOL: EDUCATION, WORK, CITIZENSHIP

What About Me

How will I tell you what I don't know
Who will help me find my way through
The dark path of shame and silence
Called school, learning, grades,
Questions asked in front of kids whose
Answers spill quickly into praise and smiles
Teachers nodding and pleased, and then
Quiet and grim as my answers fall short
Always short cuz I'm not gonna know much
And she should see me cringin' low to my seat
To avoid the disgrace facing me
Question by question

Now we're goin' to the library and how
Am I gonna figure out what to do there
How to find the destination on that computer
I know she's gonna ask things I don't know
Can't answer and all the time I'm hopin' that
She'll move far enough away so I can find
What about me in this maze of don't knows

And how can I find my way
They all are tellin' me that school is it
My way out, gettin' respectable
Ticket to a job
Family, the good life
You know what I'm sayin'

Help me, am I worth it
I dunno, maybe I could
Be somebody
It's a long shot
Teacher says there's
Way more to me than
I see
Wish I could
See who I am
Stand tall and brave
Answer the question
Know the answer
Shake hands with my
Dignity and victory

Jane Guttman

One of the biggest incentives for teens to become technologically proficient is that technology helps them prepare for the future. Whether teens plan to continue their education or enter the job market, technology skills are vital. Teens on the fringes of technology, however, are generally unaware of how technology can empower them. They may not realize or appreciate the role technology will have in their lives.

Disadvantaged teens are likely to live "in the now." They may not be able to see ahead, or they may dread the future that they *do* see. That future can seem daunting with its challenges and decision points. For the teen on the fringe, those challenges may be considered roughly parallel to Maslow's 1962 hierarchy of needs:

- *Physiological*: Where will I find shelter? How will I eat? How will I keep myself covered and warm?
- *Safety*: How will I keep safe and out of harm's way? How will I defend myself? How can I find order and stability in my surroundings?

- *Human relationships*: How can I communicate effectively with others? How can I be accepted by others? How can I establish and maintain membership in meaningful groups? How will I develop and sustain loving relationships?
- *Esteem*: How can I get the skills and knowledge set to become competent? What will I achieve? How will other people praise and admire me?
- *Self-actualization*: How can I fully realize my self-potential?

The first three levels require dependence on others; the fourth level, esteem, usually involves societal interdependence. Developmentally, all teens stand on the edge of dependent living, and they lack the means to make the break and survive more or less independently. In the process of addressing these major issues, teens also need to address secondary factors such as information literacy, economic understanding, ability to acquire material and personal assets, and interpersonal skills (Servon, 2002).

Sometimes schools do not do a thorough job of preparing teens, particularly for independent living. When teens are on the fringes of society, they are less likely to participate in formal education, take advantage of youth-serving agencies, or enter other adult networks. If they do not develop lifelong skills, these same teens may defeat themselves and live out their worst predictions: becoming homeless or dependent on others for their basic livelihood.

Today, with the incorporation of technology into so many aspects of daily adult life, teens need to be able to use technology to survive and thrive. Still, some young adults may think that technology isolates rather than connects. As teens make the transition to adult life, whether preparation for personal gain or participatory citizenship, you can help these teens to see their own potential grow through the use of technology.

JOBS/EMPLOYMENT

A quarter century ago, the U.S. Department of Health, Education and Welfare (1977) published a report about helping students make the transition to employment, postsecondary education, and other postgraduate futures. Specific tasks included providing information about careers and career preparation, identifying individual abilities and aptitudes, socializing youth for employment behaviors, offering occupational experiences, and helping students find work. The Secretary's Commission on Achieving Necessary Skills (SCANS) 1991 report further identified workforce skills:

- resources: identification, organization, planning, and allocation
- information: its acquisition and use
- systems: how they operate and interrelate
- technologies: selection, application, maintenance, and troubleshooting
- interpersonal skills

Today, technology plays a central role in the labor market—some 63 percent of jobs require technology skills. Eight out of ten of the fastest-growing industries are computer-related, and two million new information technology jobs will be created in the next ten years. Employees who use technology earn 43 percent more than others, to some extent because expertise is more difficult to attain and maintain (Children's Partnership, 2000).

While technology has been a mainstay of labor since the Industrial Revolution, new technologies such as the Internet require a more complex set of skills, and its scope and applications constantly change (Kuttan & Peters, 2003). The ability to learn on an ongoing basis certainly applies to the world of technology. On the other hand, however, women, people of color, and the disabled continue to be underrepresented in information technology careers. A serious disconnect exists.

Information Literacy and Technology

In the business world, the use of information does indeed lead to power. Ideas are considered intellectual capital and are highly valued, particularly in areas of specialized expertise that build over time. In this arena, data consist of a listing of skills that staff demonstrate; information includes the skills identified to keep competitive; knowledge enables employers to match needed skills with jobs and then train employees accordingly; and wisdom is the ability to predict needed skills and staffing. As workers migrate from job to job, building a culture of knowledge has become harder to accomplish, in that training new employees in technical positions is a very time-consuming job and fear of competition makes information-sharing riskier. Industry today is giving more attention to knowledge management: capturing human wisdom, organizing it, and developing effective mechanisms for distributing it.

In business, information literacy is often couched in terms of problem-solving and decision-making processes. Unlike most school-based learning activities though, industry solutions must factor in cost-benefit, risk levels, number of people impacted, existing biases, and company constraints. Thus, the more real world contexts for using information literacy skills that you can provide to teens, the better prepared they will be to understand the reasons for becoming information literate. School-to-work programs, in particular, focus on these skills. Programs such as these also help teens to understand and learn how to network.

Library job and career centers can meld information literacy and career exploration. As librarians, you can help teens identify job skill needs and do self-assessments. You can help students strategize career and independent living planning, provide resources, and you can refer teens to specialized reference services and career counseling. By leveraging your networking efforts with other agencies, you can develop local databases on planning for the future as well as immediate opportunities.

Communications Technology

Beyond immediate information, teens should also be exposed to technology-accessed content that helps them connect their own world to other groups, particularly the dominant economic one. In that way, teens can acquire power and gain social capital for themselves. In order to succeed as adults, teens need to prepare themselves to communicate effectively with employers and agencies that they may have use for in the future. By using technology to access content and communicate with others, teens develop new social networks that facilitate their membership into new environments. Moreover, those who continue to use the Internet tend to maintain and expand social networks of consequence, particularly if such telecommunications supplements face-to-face interaction (Strate, Jacobson, & Gibson, 2003; Warschauer, 2003).

As a librarian, you can help teens build this social capital by involving them in technology projects. As a community information center, your library can set up face-to-face introductions for teens with community and business networks. Your library can refer teens to online mentorship programs as another way to extend networking opportunities beyond the community. Similarly, organizational listservs can also be publicized so teens can engage in conversations with these professionals.

Programs for Careers and Technology

On a more general level, consider broad community-based partnerships and collaborations that help teens think about career opportunities and prepare for future goals. Developmental programs as well as career preparation services play a key role in this effort. Teens need access to safe and welcoming environments in which to explore and trusting relationships with committed staff. Programs should be stable and self-sustaining so teens can grow within that framework, and tell their younger peers about the program so that continuity can be assured.

Your library can offer relevant resources and referral information for teens as well as collaborate with community entities to provide these services. The San Francisco Public Library, for example, has an online guide for teens to identify their interests, explore possible careers, and begin preparing for their future (http://sfpl.org.sfplonline/teen/booklists/careersandeducation.htm).

The following programs also reflect the above philosophy.

Birchwood Learning Center (BLC), Operation MEDIA (Mass Education Developing Intelligent Adults)
http://www.rtpnet.org/blc/media2

Operation MEDIA is an eight-session program for teens to help them develop life skills as well as Internet and Web page design skills. Teens learn job skills, communication skills, alcohol and drug training, conflict resolution, healthy relationships, e-mail and Web page design using Netscape Composer. The program's Web page gives a program overview and specific curriculum for each lesson.

Goodwill Global Learning
http://goodwillinc.org

This charity provides online and class training on job searching, work skills, and computer skills.

HarlemLive
http://www.harlemlive.org

Teens learn Web design, video production, and business skills by producing an online magazine.

Legit
http://www.osborneny.org/employment_and_training.htm

This alternative program for incarcerated teens in Brooklyn provides counseling, educational support and mentoring, and micro-enterprises where teens learn business and entrepreneurship to partner in local business efforts.

Lynchburg (Virginia) School District Pride Center
http://www.lynchburg.org/schools/Apc/Pridemain.htm
For middle and high schoolers, this learning center provides struggling students, often truant, with nontraditional educational opportunities. It provides software and online courses matched with individual student needs, and helps older students get work experience that they can balance with their academic subjects.

Plugged In Enterprises
http://www.pluggedin.org/pie/index.html
An East Palo Alto (California) youth-operated design firm that produces high-quality, custom-tailored Web and graphic services.

Technical Teens Internship Program
http://www.techaccess.orgttip/ttipoverview.aspx
This program is for teens ages 14 to 18. They are given advanced information technology training in preparation for paid summer internships that will lead to careers in Information Technology or other highly technical fields.

Youth Entertainment Summer Program
http://www.yestojobs.org
Y.E.S. is an opportunity for minority high school students to spend ten weeks employed in entry-level positions at communications businesses.

The following Web-based Internet sites target teens, often those who are traditionally underserved.

All About Work
http://www.nhlink.net/employme/
Local job information is provided on this site as well as helpful answers to employment questions in a simple format.

Black Enterprise
http://www.blackenterprise.com
This site addresses business issues and includes the best colleges for Blacks.

Hotshot Business
www.disney.go.com/hotshot
Disney developed a simulation of business development for 9 to 12-year-olds.

Pathfinder Science
http://pathfinderscience.net
This virtual community for teachers practices mutual respect, embraces diversity, and inspires a passion for learning about the material world through science.

Plugged In
http://www.pluggedin.org/index.html
East Palo Alto (California) developed a community network that includes a youth entrepreneurship program.

Preparing for Successful Telementoring Relationships
http://techlearning.com/db_area/archives/WCE/archives/tsikalas.htm
Kallen Tsikalas describes two telementoring projects she worked on, which were conducted by the Center for Children and Technology. Citing project examples and relevant literature, she discusses the nature of mentoring and ways to optimize the process.

Teens 4 Hire
http://www.teens4hire.org
This search engine helps teens find jobs online.

YoungBiz
http://youngbiz.com/
This site offers entrepreneurial ideas for young people. Profiles of young entrepreneurs and message boards are also part of this site. In addition, it provides educational information about business concepts, especially those related to investment.

FURTHER EDUCATION

In traditional societies, young people learned by doing. Apprenticeship was a normal way to learn a skill and enter a profession. Nowadays, while some specific skills are still learned on the job, most employers look for people who are literate and have a general educational background. Certainly, jobs that entail technology require some sort of advanced training. Nevertheless, for some at-risk teens, a four-year high school experience is out of the picture, either because of circumstances or hard choices they have made. Still, getting a General Education Diploma (GED) is possible—and technology can facilitate that goal, as well as other goals.

Overall, goal setting and planning impacts participation in education—and technology use. Interestingly, in a recent survey of college-bound, high school students, little or no digital divide was discerned along ethnic lines. Ninety-four percent of white students had home access to technology; 91 percent of African Americans did. At school, the picture was slightly different: 81 percent among whites and 71 percent among African Americans. On the other hand, those students who did not have college plans tended to reflect a greater ethnic discrepancy. The findings imply that family support and expectations may well impact student academic success (Carlson, 2003). Too often, minorities or at-risk teens have little information or hold misinformation about college, so do not plan for such opportunities. Ideally, they should have placement exams in high school to get an idea of colleges' expectations and have opportunities to experience college courses early on. High school dropouts might not realize the usefulness of a GED or know how to earn one.

Technology can help in these endeavors. Computer-aided instruction can help teens hone basic skills and advance cognitive development. Simulations and open-ended software programs, as well as educational Web sites, can foster constructivist learning. Several states and commercial enterprises are pursuing distance-learning models for high schoolers so teens can take advanced courses that are not offered locally. These technology-based approaches can work well with at-risk teens who do not feel comfortable with the traditional school structure.

For those teens who need to work or must keep nonschool hours, technology-rich learning venues can provide needed instruction at their convenience. Furthermore, teens can work at their own pace and gain more control over their education, which may motivate them to seek advanced training.

As a model, the PLUS (Positive Links Between Universities and Schools) Project for older young adults (15- to 20-year-olds) at the computer lab at Queensland University of Technology (Australia) showcases people of color to model and speak about their use of technology for work and personal gain; they also share their favorite Web sites. As a result, teens see literacy as a social practice embedded in cultural experiences. Teens in this program use e-mail, have ethnic tutors, and access to experts and peers. The project also incorporates literacy activities, such as reading different types of texts. The program encourages students to contribute to the electronic community by sharing Aboriginal culture with students around the world (Doherty, 2002).

High school, college, and public libraries can support advanced education by making available resources on higher education, database subscriptions, educational portals, and workshops on lifelong learning. Below are a few good programs and Web sites that address these issues.

College Cost Central
http://edworkforce.house.gov/issues/108th/education/highereducation/collegecostcentral.htm
Shows college costs and how to meet them.

College Net
http://www.collegenet.com/
A portal for applying for college over the Web.

Double Discovery Center
http://www.columbia.edu/cu/college/ddc/

College-preparatory program to develop, design, and enhance education and technology-oriented learning environments for more than 900 disadvantaged students, parents, volunteers and staff.

GearUp
http://www.ed.gov/gearup
Government information on funding and materials to help teens get ready for college. It is geared toward those teens whose goal it is to enter the science and engineering fields.

La Clase Magica, University of California San Diego
http://communication.ucsd.edu/LCM
Disadvantaged young people are given access to high-end technology and a supportive learning environment.

Your ABC
http://yourabc.com
This site has links to education, particularly advice on higher education and online learning.

CITIZENSHIP/POLITICS

Thomas Jefferson said that the best insurance for democracy was an informed citizenry. Ongoing civic participation is therefore an important part of adult life. Informed decisions about governmental action should be based on the facts and be representative of all citizens' expectations and needs. As societies become more pluralistic, all voices need to be heard—and all social entities need to know the realities of their communities.

Today's teens are not typically engaged in political action. Fewer than 20 percent have ever contacted a political figure. Voting among 18-year-olds has declined during the past four decades. Young people prefer to support causes instead or make their civic voices heard on local issues, where they feel they have more say in the outcome. Interestingly, girls are more likely to be engaged in civic activities and think they can make a difference.

Furthermore, teens in heterogeneous communities were more likely to get involved in civic action than those in homogeneous neighborhoods (Gimpel, Lay, & Schuknecht, 2003). Still, African Americans and Latinos feel that they have less impact on political issues than Anglos, and they also have less trust in the government: Both perceptions correlate with less civic engagement. Other factors that positively influence teen civic participation are parental participation in civic action and religious activities (Center for Information and Research on Civic Learning and Engagement, 2002).

Technologically disadvantaged teens might not be aware of civic issues or realize how they can impact them. If their time and effort are already stretched due to immediate demands, the thought of civic responsibility may seem abstract or unnecessary. Politically disengaged teens are not likely to seek political information on the Net. Other teens may consider governmental agencies and representatives as the enemy and feel that they are being victimized by the powerful. However, even if teens do not like those perceived oppressors, they should learn enough about civic institutions to be able to confront issues knowledgeably, offer alternative directions, and advocate for community needs and content. Taking political action in itself is empowering, whether the goals are met or not.

Fortunately, with the advent of the Internet, a virtual political system is emerging, which can lead to active citizenship and engagement (Norris, 2001). Instant information is now available by a broad spectrum of interests. The Internet provides an interactive environment where teens can receive and give timely feedback about issues they feel strongly about. The Internet offers a way to democratize ideas and give the populace a voice. Typically, people gravitate to special interest groups and social movements. In some cases, grassroots efforts can "seed" participation. An online community may develop quickly and can be structured to leverage lobbying and advocacy and ultimately make an impact governmental policies.

Indeed, a two-year study by the Center for Social Media (Ailworth, 2004) examined 300 civic-related Web sites geared to Generation Y (i.e., persons born since 1979). During the lead up to the 2004 election, Howard Dean's grassroots Internet presidential campaign was the most visible example of Web-related organizing. Other sites such as MoveOn.org provided viable ways to advocate for change and participate in community activism. Another site that offers an interactive forum for young people to voice their opinions on issues of the day is www.YouthOutlook.org. A Web site that lists volunteer opportunities is www.Idealist.org (Ailworth, 2004).

On the downside, large corporations and lobbying groups, such as the National Rifle Association, can crowd the Internet with their own agendas, sometimes hiding behind a benign front. Smaller groups often get lost in the flurry, splinter, or have short-range goals. Political Internet enthusiasts tend to want freedom and control and generally support alternative social movements on the outer edges of the political scene. For that reason, teens need to critically evaluate political messages on the Web.

Libraries have traditionally served as neutral town halls of information. In the age of technology, your library can continue to fulfill this role by providing the same kind of balanced information online. Your library Web pages can focus on community or other civic issues and provide a means for constituents to voice their opinions and justify their actions. A social network can be built and then fortified with face-to-face projects. You can enlist teens in this endeavor by having them videotape public events, conduct political interviews on audiotape, survey other teens about their civic needs, and develop issues-specific Web pages. By using these existing structures, you can help teens champion their own social and political causes.

Consider the following projects that exemplify successful outreach to teens for civic engagement.

Center for Civic Networking
http://www.civicnet.org
This site fosters citizen participation in government and community development through information infrastructures.

Community Information Agents Online (CIAO)
http://flint.lib.mi.us/flintprofiles/index.html
An intensive after-school community technology program that fosters teen civic engagement by giving them the skills they need to help a community organization as it developed a Web presence.

Digital Clubhouse Network
http://www.digiclub.org
This site teaches teens responsible citizenship through technology training to improve the quality of life in their community and includes service projects.

Youth Vote Coalition
http://www.youthvote.org
A national nonpartisan coalition of diverse organizations dedicated to increasing political and civic participation among young people.

TARGETED TEENS ON THE FRINGES OF THE FUTURE

All teens need to be prepared for the future, but some teens have traditionally been disadvantaged in this endeavor: inner-city youth, girls, and teens with disabilities. Their issues vary greatly, so one solution will not fit all. Each group shares some common issues, so those elements can be addressed systematically. Within that framework, technology can be used as a worthwhile "hook" to get teens access to skills and to become forward thinking. Of course, you must be sensitive to each group's unique factors relating to norms, background, interests, and learning preferences.

Inner-City Youth

Urban youth face several issues relative to their future. One major issue focuses on personal expectations: higher education might not be highly valued among their peers, and girls may look for self-fulfillment through marriage or motherhood rather than academics. Those teens who make a conscious decision to make career plans may lack the social assets they need to deal with their future. Because of poverty they may lack access to community resources due to limited networking options or fee-based services. Immigrants may derive their ideas of social services from their original country and therefore do not pursue services that they may be eligible for at no cost; they may also fear deportation and thus avoid contact with governmental agencies. Additionally, some teens may be extra-sensitive to snubs by others, particularly by those in power, and then react negatively, thus leading to a vicious cycle of miscommunication and missed opportunities (Besharov, 1999). In the final analysis, these teens may well feel that they cannot control their future.

While politics exist about library functions, still, each user has a great say in how to take advantage of the library's resources and services in terms of career exploration. As mentioned before, the library is one of the few public places that can provide free access to technology. At the very least, your library can display resources and host programs about technology as it applies to independent living issues and career options, making sure that local speakers connect with at-risk teens. As you get to know teens on a personal level, you can ask them to help out or give advice relative to technology and career planning. One-shot activities may be more appropriate for these teens to "test the library waters" and for you to see if a good "fit" exists between teen and program; however, building a foundation for longer-term interaction can help teens develop employment skills and provide evidence of work that can lead to employment—including librarianship.

Girls

Schools do not always provide equal learning experiences for girls and boys relative to technology. In Silverman and Pritchard's study of technology use in middle schools (1999), they observed that technology-enhanced project topics were either gender neutral or inherently of more interest to boys than girls (e.g., cars, machines). Girls were discouraged from taking advanced technology courses; furthermore, girls did not want to risk being outnumbered by boys.

From 1989 to 1999, the percentage of girls taking the Advanced Placement (AP) computer tests rose only 1 percent, from 16 percent to 17 percent, and of the 6 percent who identified computers or information science as their major, only 23 percent were girls, and they scored significantly lower than boys. Fewer than 34 percent of math and computer science majors are female, down 25 percent since 1989.

In terms of career exploration, girls tended to lack information about the impact of technology on salaries and promotions. Instead, they were inclined to classify all technology jobs as masculine (Silverman & Pritchard, 1999). Ironically, the U.S. Department of Commerce (2002) found that women use technology in the workplace more than men across all age groups.

What can be done? In its 2003 report about information technology in education relative to girls, UNICEF made several recommendations:

- use information and communication technology as an end to a means, not an end in itself
- use the Internet to collect information and collaborate
- use the Internet to foster an interactive learning environment
- promote cross-site communication via the Internet

These issues and recommendations can be addressed effectively by school libraries by providing access and information about technology. As a gateway to information, school libraries can facilitate career exploration that addresses girls' interests. The use of technology in the library can focus on information literacy and research steps that encourage problem solving and decision making. School librarians, who are primarily female, can model technology use and train female library aides to use technology effectively.

The following Web sites offer technology-related career sites targeted to girls.

Girl Geeks
http://www.girlgeeks.org/education/resources.shtml
Educational technology resources and programs.

Girls for a Change
http://www.girlsforachange.org
Originating in SiliconValley, this program builds on girls' societal awareness and ability to collaborate by facilitating community-based improvement projects that incorporate technology.

Girls in Technology
http://www.girlsintechnology.org
Targeted to socially disadvantaged girls in metropolitan Washington, DC, this program provides career exploration activities and mentoring.

Ignite-us
http://www.ignite-us.org
A partnership between the Seattle School District and local technology industries to "inspire girls now in technology evolution" through industry visits and mentoring with professional women. The organization also sponsors an e-zine created for and by high school girls.

Telementoring Young Women in Engineering and Computing: Providing the Vital Link
http://www2.edc.org/CCT/projects_summary.asp?numProjectId=771
An experimental project funded by the National Science Foundation that is designed to link female high school students interested in the sciences, engineering, and computing to adult women mentors via the Internet.

Web sites for Girls
http://research.umbc.edu/~korenman/wmst/links_girls.html
The University of Maryland's links for girls about technology and related careers.

Teens with Disabilities

Preparing for education and employment can be challenging for teens with disabilities. They may already feel isolated and may not have a strong social network to help them get ready for independent life. At the most basic level, these teens need to feel safe living in their community, be able to stand up for themselves, and identify and use available resources (Greene & Kochhar-Bryant, 2003).

Only one-third of adults with disabilities are working at any point, and women with disabilities have far less chance of being hired than their male counterparts. Moreover, women, African Americans, and Latinos with disabilities earn less per hour than their Anglo peers. Ironically, of those adults with disabilities who are employed, 69 percent asserted that they did not need special accommodations to work effectively (Greene & Kochhar-Bryant, 2003). When the issue of technology arises, these same populations tend to have less access and less knowledge than other populations. Since so many jobs require technical skills, it is imperative that teens with disabilities get technical training so they will have a better chance for economic success.

Teens with disabilities have several employment options: dedicated sheltered workshops, supported work crews for highly structured jobs, supported individual employment, and competitive employment (Greene & Kochhar-Bryant, 2003). Training for these different venues ranges from developmental and repetitive training with constant supervision to community-based, employment skills focused in a mainstreamed environment. Much of the training success depends as much on the potential employer as it does on the young adult; perceptions can influence efforts and success significantly.

Again, technology can play a role in training and placement. Resources that can help develop needed skills include educational computer programs and videotapes, telecommunications, and relevant Web sites. Adult coaching can provide the focused structure that these teens need and can help them learn how to use these resources collaboratively and independently. Probably the two greatest motivators are a sense of empowerment and being accepted as a participant in a meaningful social activity. The diagnostic and interactive features of high-quality relevant digital programs also provide the immediate feedback and structure that benefits this group of teens.

The following programs and Web sites describe effective ways to help teens with disabilities prepare for the future.

Association for Persons in Supported Employment
http://www.apse.org
This group focuses on the vocational needs of individuals with disabilities.

National Center on Secondary Education and Transition
http://ncset.org
Helps teens with disabilities prepare for high school and the workplace.

Partners On-Line E-Mentoring Program for Youth with Disabilities
http://www.pyd.org/
An e-mentoring program serving youth and young adults with disabilities by using e-mail, online conferences/meetings, chat rooms, and one-to-one online discussions with each other, their parents, and business mentors.

U.S. Disability Law
http://www.law.cornell.edu/topics/disability.html
Discusses laws that protect the rights of people with disabilities.

In short, at-risk teens may think they have little to look forward to. As they cope with immediate crises, it may seem foolhardy to plan ahead. In some cases, these teens may be confusing "future" with "options." Still, the future *will* come, whether they are ready to deal with it. Likewise, technology will also be part of their future. If schools emphasize a traditional educational approach and disregard their at-risk students, these young people will feel that they do not have a meaningful role in society; they will have nothing to lose if they drop out or rebel.

As public institutions, libraries can offer another, more positive picture for youth. You can help them solve present-day problems by using information technology, and show them how those solutions can pave the way to lifelong skills. As librarians, you can help them see how their present interests and capabilities can lead to satisfying and financially successful careers by planning appropriate ways to enhance their education using technology. By tapping into teens' frustrations about society's problems and showing them how to leverage technology to make their voices heard, they can work to improve their community. In modeling effective ways to use technology, you can bridge the present to a promising tomorrow.

WORKS CITED

Ailworth, E. (2004, March 23). On the Web, Gen-Y and civic duty click. *Los Angeles Times,* E10.

Besharov, D. (Ed.). (1999). *America's disconnected youth.* Washington, DC: CWLA Press.

Carlson, S. (2003, May 2). Firm's survey of college-bound students finds no digital divide among them. *The Chronicle of Higher Education, 49* (34), A37.

Center for Information and Research on Civic Learning and Engagement. (2002). *Youth civic engagement.* Washington, DC: CIRCLE.

The Children's Partnership. (2000). *Online content for low-income and underserved Americans.* Santa Monica, CA: The Children's Partnership. http://www.childrenspartnership.org/pub/low_income/index.html.

Doherty, C. (2002, September). Extending horizons: Critical technological literacy for urban Aboriginal students. *Journal of Adolescent & Adult Literacy, 46*(1), 50–59.

Gimpel, J., Lay, J., & Schuknecht, J. (2003). *Cultivating democracy: Civic environments and political socialization in America.* Washington, DC: Brookings Institution Press.

Greene, G., & Kochhar-Bryant, C. (2003). *Pathways to successful transition for youth with disabilities.* Upper Saddle River, NJ: Merrill.

Kuttan, A., & Peters, L. (2003). *From digital divide to digital opportunity.* Lanham, MD: Scarecrow Press.

Maslow, A. (1962). *Toward a psychology of being.* Princeton, NJ: Van Nostrand.

Norris, P. (2001). *Digital divide: Civic engagement, information poverty, and the Internet worldwide.* Cambridge, MA: Cambridge University Press.

Secretary's Commission on Achieving Necessary Skills. (1991). *What work requires of schools: A SCANS report for America 2000.* Washington, DC: Department of Labor.

Servon, L. (2002). *Bridging the digital divide: Technology, community, and public policy.* Oxford: Blackwell.

Silverman, S. & Pritchard, A. (1996, September). Building their future: Girls and technology education in Connecticut. *Journal of Technology Education, 7*(2). http://scholar.lib.vt.edu/ejournals/JTE/v7n2/silverman.jte-v7n2.htm.

Strate, L., Jacobson, J., & Gibson, S. (Eds.). (2003). *Communication and cyberspace: Social interaction in an electronic environment.* (2nd ed.). Cresskill, NJ: Hampton Press.

UNICEF. (2003). *Girls' education: Focus on technology.* New York: UNICEF.

U.S. Department of Commerce. (2002). *A nation online: How Americans are expanding their use of the Internet.* Washington, DC: U.S. Department of Commerce. http://www.ntia.doc.gov/ntiahome/dn/.

Warschauer, M. (2003). *Technology and social inclusion: Rethinking the digital divide.* Cambridge, MA: MIT Press.

4

PERCEPTIONS OF TECHNOLOGY

Quick!
Do you know me?
I'm strugglin' to live through the day
So what is technology anyway?
I'm not some white boy with allowance
Or a fat wallet
Quick!
Find me if you can
Hidin' in some box or
Smelly place
And show me how to *get*
Technology . . .
Quick!
I'm dyin' and I haven't
Even lived . . .

Jane Guttman

Quick! What image comes to mind when you envision the term "technology user"? Chances are it's Bill Gates or some other Anglo male adult. How does a Latina teen relate to those images?

When the Bureau of Labor Statistics (2004) asserts that three-quarters of jobs involve technology, do visions of flat screens or Cray computers arise? For teens with limited technological knowledge and experience, nightmares of McDonald's cash registers are more likely.

If teens are resistant to technology and unaware of its benefits, or if they have had negative experiences with technology, they are less prone to pursue access and take advantage of it for their own self-improvement.

Likewise, misconceptions and stereotypes about technology can lead to its underutilization by the very populations who could most benefit from it. One of the problems is that technology is often considered a tool rather than a means of social information communication and use. The same teens who brush-off computers as number-crunching machines may spend hours on their cell phones. In addition, when technology is linked with mathematics, teens who flunked algebra may decide never to touch a keyboard.

In short, teens on the fringes of technology need to find out about it and experience it positively, yet they are often on the fringes of education as well, so traditional means of informing them often miss the target.

COMMON MISCONCEPTIONS ABOUT TECHNOLOGY AND WHO HAS THEM

Most teens today are aware of technology in general, via television and the media, but they may not be aware of its diversity or the extent to which it can be used to further their own economic and daily lives. Interestingly, lower-income families tend to use computers more for entertainment and self-improvement, while higher-income families use computers for a greater range of activities (Attewell, 2001). Part of this situation rises from parents who do not know some of the educational benefits of technology or who fear what their youngsters may find on the Internet (McNabb et al., 1999). Some girls reject computers because they dislike its connotations of violent video games and geekdom (American Association of University Women, 2000). In short, perceptions about technology are often societally contextualized.

Technology is part of most schools' curricula, but teens who are out of public education are less likely to know about it. New immigrants who have not had prior experience are unlikely to know about the extent of technology or how to access it. Since most content on the Internet is in English, non-English speakers and readers might not see how technology relate to them. Those who are illiterate, U.S.- or foreign-born, may associate technology with the Internet, which has been largely textual in nature, or with education where they have experienced failure. Most people who are unaware of technology, then, have not seen or experienced it.

WHY SHOULD TEENS CARE ABOUT TECHNOLOGY?

Technology can broaden the gap between people or bring them together. Its use can advance those with power or leave the rest behind or it can help level the socioeconomic playing field. Those same teens who see technology as the Other may fail to see that technology can help them improve their own lot.

Technology is not just a tool for making financial investments online, or for belonging to a literary chat group. Technology provides multiple benefits for teens on the fringes of society: physically, educationally, economically, and politically. These benefits include:

- information and assistance about: news, weather, people, transportation, jobs, education, health, parenting, social services, immigration/citizenship, consumerism, politics
- expert help for: homework, need for language translation, legal issues
- financial help for: record-keeping, banking, scholarships, job leads, comparison shopping
- social and career networking
- communications vehicle using a variety of formats (particularly attractive to immigrants who want to keep in touch with their homeland at little cost)
- creation/production tools
- entertainment: sports, music, video, anime, writing, images
- assistance and compensatory tools for the physically challenged
- technical skills to aid in all the above

So why do some teens lack enthusiastism about technology? When they do not feel safe in school, when there is no home to go to, when life itself seems like a question mark, then technology does not seem very relevant (Wessler, 2003). If technology is associated with Game Boy or a single period in school where teens do flashcards via computer, then technology may seem childish and condescending (Dooling, 2000). If, on top of that, technology is pictured as a geeky toy for white boys with time and money on their hands, if it is regarded as another consumer product, then technology does not seem like a desirable thing to pursue (Wilhelm, 2001). A 2003 Pew study found that the percentage of Internet users in the United States (58 percent) has leveled off in the past year, and that at the same time that new users come on board, others have dropped out because of negative experiences (e.g., lack of literacy or computer skills, mechanical problems, lack of relevant content). These nonusers tend to be poorer, less educated, and feel less in control of their surroundings (Lenhart, 2003).

Sometimes teens do not realize the extent to which technology has become part of their lives. In fact, technology is all around us. More households have televisions than have refrigerators. Cars and Barbie dolls both have computer chips. Cell phones are used by people of all ages and economic backgrounds—even by the homeless, who use them as a stable "address."

Public services as well as private enterprises rely on technology for information and its processing. Employers expect technological competence of new hires. Today, political and social movements are using the Internet to make a difference. Technology has facilitated globalization, which daily impacts the U.S. economy. Today's world is truly wired (Warschauer, 2003, p. 1). The message we need to convey is, Technology is all around you, so deal with it and turn it to your advantage.

Often, disenfranchised teens do not get equitable social services. They are dealing with issues of survival, health, and safety. Telecommunications can help teens get health information and access to local public agencies. Information may be general, such as advice about eating disorders or depression, or community-specific, such as HIV testing locations. Parenting and personal advice are also available and free and can help avoid life crises; for example, Young Mommies Help Site (http://www.youngmommies.com) is a safe resource for teen mothers and mothers-to-be to obtain advice and share their stories, and online crisis lines offer confidential and anonymous support (http://teenadvice.about.com/od/crisislinesadvice). With translation programs and information in non-English languages, literate immigrants can find out about available social programs. Many special interest groups, ranging from homeless to transgender advocates, can help individual teens who might otherwise feel reluctant to ask for help.

Disabled teens benefit greatly from technology as they learn to access information and communicate with others. However, this population has been underrepresented in terms of technology use, mainly because of cost. With the appropriate assistive technology, these teens can take advantage of multimedia files to compensate for physical limitations (e.g., information can be read aloud for the visually impaired), and for the first time they can demonstrate their own knowledge so others can understand them. Furthermore, on the Internet teens with disabilities can chat with and support each other.

Online information and instruction enables teens to access needed information outside of school strictures and social prejudice. Both television and the Internet provide anonymity and autonomy. The Internet has the added advantage of being interactive so teens can control how they retrieve information. They can connect with experts, and get appropriate feedback that helps them learn more effectively and efficiently. Web-based learning can also help teens connect with a new set of peers, thus extending their social network.

Learning how to use technology can open economic doors for teens now and in the future. Teens can apply for jobs online, and search for companies that are a good fit with their own qualifications. They can find free Web tutorials to learn technology skills. They can present their ideas professionally by learning how to do desktop publishing. By using technology, teens can create a new social identity, which can open new networking doors.

Teens may also feel powerless against social injustice. Using video as well as digital technologies, teens gain the opportunity to tell their stories and agitate for social change. They can write to government agencies and officials. They can publish their points of view in print and nonprint media. With local public access required of all cable stations as well as low-cost Web-hosting opportunities, teens can reach local or international audiences with their causes.

In short, technology can help build traditional and innovative social capital: a means to connect with spheres of influence and make positive contributions. The Internet, in particular, attracts people who want to advance their personal interests as well as those who want to promote community activism (Katz, Rice, & Aspden, 2002).

GETTING THE WORD OUT

As librarians, you understand that free access to information is a public good, and that informed and educated citizens improve the social welfare of the public as a whole. You also realize that technology expands the world of information and helps its dissemination. Most libraries seek to serve *all* people, and librarians understand that teenagers constitute one quarter of the population that uses public libraries. Libraries need to serve teens, so they can make good use of the libraries' facilities—and support them throughout their lives.

Although some of the causes of the digital divide are lack of awareness and inaccurate perceptions, it makes sense for libraries to educate and inform the teen population about technology and its benefits so they will become motivated to access and use the library. Often, those who are unaware of what technology has to offer are also unaware of what libraries have to offer. Thus, libraries have to "sell their product"—library services in general and technology in particular—to nonusers.

Before you undertake outreach efforts, make sure your technology is sufficient and supported by your own Web site. Nothing creates a backlash more than promising a service and then not being able to deliver it. Remember talking about a great book, and then having only one copy on the shelf, thus frustrating a classroom of enchanted listeners? A negative experience can turn off a teenager for years to come. The same principle applies to technology. If you assert that teens can gain personal and economic power through technology, then the hardware and software at your library—as well as the Internet connectivity—had better be in place. Teens will be turned off by old, beat-up equipment, slow access speed, and narrow bandwidth. They do not like waiting in line to use a computer, or being kicked off the system after fifteen minutes.

Teens like to chat online, so either allow that function, or make it very clear from the beginning that such services will not be available. In short, do not advertise anything that you cannot deliver.

Moreover, be sure that training and support are available in case teens need help. Ideally, someone should be around to help teens when they get stuck. Having a teen serve as a tech coach can help other teens save face and provide help from someone who speaks their language, literally and figuratively. Simple how-to posters and reference sheets with clear diagrams can provide ready reference. Online help screens or tutorials can assist in just-in-time troubleshooting for more experienced users. The same written and online instructions can be produced for teen and adult patrons, so ideally only one person in the library system or district needs to be able to provide these documents. On the other hand, tech aides need to be recruited, trained, and supervised by youth-serving librarians in order to build the personal and trusting relationship that is so important in working with this age group.

Finally, remember that your library is only as successful as your personnel. The best equipment and connectivity cannot overcome unpleasant and tech-ignorant staff, so make sure that your staff members are tech-savvy and effective at training teens about technology upon request. Your staff should also be linguistically representative of the community you serve.

A systematic approach to raising awareness maximizes your library's impact in the community. The following steps can help you in this process:

1. Know your community. Conduct a needs assessment about teens and technology. Observe teens in action. Talk with them, inside and outside of the library. It may be hard to contact the very teens whom you want to attract to the library, so data gathering might have to start by focusing on the communities in which these teens live. Cull information from existing records: census, schools, newspapers, public agencies. If you are a public librarian, visit your local middle and high schools and see what kind of computer equipment they have, what training they offer, and what is missing. Talk with representatives of community agencies and organizations, particularly those entities that serve targeted teens or their families: youth groups, recreation directors, social workers, correctional officers, church leaders, school personnel, and public health and hospital personnel. Some businesses and organizations have community liaisons or customer service agents who can provide valuable information while keeping teen confidentiality. And find out where technology exists—or, more important, where it is lacking; for example, public utilities know where telecommunications lines have been dropped for Internet connectivity. Even a telephone directory might list businesses that provide public access to technology. By learning about your community, you can find out which populations have the greatest needs for technology.
2. Identify your target audience. Because students are more likely to know about technology than those who have dropped out of school, public libraries should make a special effort to reach that sector of young adults. Some teens who are in school, however, are also on the fringe, so efforts in the schools, particularly those that are underfunded, should also be supported. Additionally, because teens of color, particularly Latinos/as, are more likely to drop out earlier, libraries should target them directly; possible venues in-

clude church bulletins, local radio stations, notices in beauty parlors and shopping malls, among other places. English language learners and illiterates are also likely audiences who need to hear your message. Work through community agencies, such as ESL and GED programs, or social services agencies to identify your audience and make contact with them. Because each group probably has a unique set of conditions and barriers, your message needs to be customized in order to attract their attention.

3. Identify audience motivators. With all technologies, and especially the Internet, the primary attractions are interaction with people and access to information (Katz, Rice, & Aspden, 2002). Build on those natural appeals. Specific motivating factors include obtaining contact information to help with survival issues, personal advice, nontraditional education, and employment. In general, look at ways to help teens feel safe and healthy, provide a means for them to connect with others, and help them feel good about themselves and in control of their lives. Indeed, technology can be a motivating factor to visit the library; that is, teens are often more attracted to technology than they are to libraries, so making them aware of technology can actually build teen awareness. A good way to appeal to teenage parents is through free story hours, particularly if they are conducted in the primary language of the parents.
4. Develop compelling messages. Use the information garnered from the needs assessment to fine tune the message that attract teens. Being "cool" is important. Teens want a quality product, and they want something that is valued by their peers. Note that 90 percent of teens think that the Internet is "in" (Meyers, 1999). Here are some taglines using the "American Library Association @your library" campaign (http://www.ala.org/ala/pio/campaign/campaignamericas.htm) that might resonate with teens on the fringe:
   - Work smart @your library
   - Access the world @your library
   - Find a job @your library
   - It's not just academic @your library
   - Sound advice @your library
   - Get an education @your library
   - Something for everyone @your library

- Many faces, many voices @your library
- Leer en tu biblioteca

For teens who read in another language, the following Web site has graphics that send the same message in over a dozen world languages: http://www.ifla.org/@yourlibrary/index.htm.

Within the broad framework of technology, specific messages may be generated, such as:

- a world of music at your fingertips
- connecting to the world through the Internet
- networking to find your "space"
- finding your video voice
- get skilled, get hired, get money—for free
- Are you a single mom? AND a teen? You're only a click away from a friend

Local, customized "branding" efforts may be a better match for teens who distrust cookie-cutter or establishment blandness. Appealing to a sense of community, messages might have a neighborhood flavor:

See how TET is celebrated "back home" @your library.

Make your grunge band famous @your library.

Eternalize the voices of your Elders @your library.

While sample slogans have been provided here, longer messages might be needed to explain the library's intent. Moreover, messages can take several forms, not just in print and not just in English.

5. Determine how to deliver your message. Internet messages will not reach teens who are unaware of or resistant to technology. Therefore, choose those media to which teens are already loyal: television and radio Public Service Announcements (PSA), window displays in stores, printed flyers and ads on public transportation and in public areas, articles in local or ethnic newspapers and magazines, motivational speakers who resonate with teens (i.e., successful business people, entertainers and other public figures, community leaders, young parents), community word-of-mouth teen library users.

   Where are teens likely to encounter your message—and trust it? The answers might be found in music stores, video gaming centers, beaches, sports arenas, fast-food restaurants, community bulletin boards, local radio stations, social services agencies, drug rehab facilities, movie theaters, and shopping malls. Your message should also be in sync with the places where the messages are posted, so teens can make natural connections, such as a flyer about library videotaping workshops at a video rental outlet. Check those establishments to make sure they are reputable and credible with teens; take the time to talk with the owners to find out more about the teens who use their services and to explain how your library might be able to work collaboratively with them.

Timing and frequency also have an impact on your message. Usually, it is more effective to send a series of consistent messages over a period of time than to deliver a one-time message or a variety of messages simultaneously to the same audience. The same message might be sent in different formats or different languages to match teens' communications preferences. For example, Latinas may be looking for *fotonovelas* or Asians may be seeking *anime*.

Also, consider collaborating with other groups in order to get out your message. What institutions or individuals do your targeted teens respect and use: churches, markets, entertainers, sports figures, social workers, parole officers, public health nurses? It is more effective to build on successful groups than to create new ones. In addition, focus groups can provide valuable information about effective delivery methods and also get participants to act as technology advocates. Consider getting the advice of professional advertisers, especially if those agencies have local ties to the community.

Think about doing "tech-talks," similar to booktalks, but focusing on and demonstrating what technology can do for teens—sharing anecdotes, success stories, and so on—in schools, at detention facilities, at teen gatherings, and so forth.

6. Evaluate the message and the process. Try to find out if your messages were effective. Evaluate which ones were the most productive by asking teens and examining library usage (i.e., program attendance, in-house use of technology, the number of printouts, library portal "hits," circulation of nonprint materials). For instance, if teens attend a workshop or program, ask them how they found out about the activity. If teens request time to use the computers, ask them how they knew that the library provided that service. Also try using technology to get the answers; incorporate simple

interactive survey forms on the computer "splash screen" to find out if the users are new or repeat users, and how they learned about the library's technology. You can also chat with teens in the library or other public areas to get their perspective on technology in the library. Content analysis of the library's systems—Internet site histories and network directory use—can also provide rich data about users, although linking portal analysis directly to teen users is problematic unless Web sites are teen-centric or timing is such that only teens were connected. By finding out how teens gather information, you can hone your message and communications channels to optimize results. Moreover, by determining which technology applications are the most important, you can build a stable foundation of teen users.

THE BIG PICTURE

While the emphasis in this chapter has been on developing focused messages for specific technology programs and services, the concept of a library message is much broader. Your message may be an enduring mission or core value. Thus, in the context of this book, one of your library's core missions is to help teens have a better life through the effective use of technology; that is the ultimate message. As your library strives to carry out that mission, each of the strategies has its own, more specific message. Every strategic message should align with the overarching mission, just as each service in the library should align with your library's vision.

Making teens aware of technology and building appreciation and interest in it requires complex planning, marketing, and evaluation: from delivering a targeted message to individual teens, for example, to establishing the library's overall mission. A systematic approach is a good investment of time because it maximizes the library's ability to reach underserved teens and work with them to provide meaningful technology experiences that can lead to a better future for them and their community.

WORKS CITED

American Association of University Women. (2000). *Tech-savvy: Educating girls in the new computer age.* Washington, DC: AAUW.

Attewell, P. (2001, July). The first and second digital divides. *Sociology of Education, 74*(3), 252–259.

Bureau of Labor Statistics. (2004). *Tomorrow's Jobs*. Washington, DC: U.S. Department of Labor.

Dooling, J. (2000, October). What students want to learn about computers. *Educational Leadership, 58*(2), 20–24.

Katz, J., Rice, R., & Aspden, P. (2001, November). The Internet, 1995–2000: Access, civic involvement, and social interaction. *American Behavioral Scientist, 45*(3), 405–419.

Lenhart, A. (2003). *The ever-shifting Internet population: A new look at Internet access and the digital divide.* Washington, DC: The Pew Internet and American Life Project. http://www.pewinternet.org/pdfs/PIP_Shifting_Net_Pop_Report.pdf.

McNabb, M., et al. (1999). *Technology connections for school improvement planner's handbook.* Naperville, IL: North Central Regional Educational Laboratory.

Meyers, E. (1999). The coolness factor: Ten libraries listen to youth. *American Libraries, 30*(10), 42–45.

U.S. Department of Health, Education, and Welfare. (1977). *Federal policy on education and work.* Washington, DC: Government Printing Office.

Warschauer, M. (2003). *Technology and social inclusion: Rethinking the digital divide.* Cambridge, MA: MIT Press.

Wessler, S. (2003, September). It's hard to learn when you're scared. *Educational Leadership, 61*(1), 40–43.

Wilhelm, A. (2001, April). They threw me a computer . . . but what I really needed was a life preserver. *First Monday, 6*(4). http://firstmonday.org/issues/issue6_4/wilhelm/index.html.

5

PHYSICAL ACCESS TO TECHNOLOGY

Don't forget about me . . .
I don't have no computer
Nor even a backpack
Sixteen going on sixty
If you count my experience
No drug I don't know
Lost my virginity at 12
Parents in jail
Not much money
Or food
In a dark hour
I know there's a way out
My alternative school
Has computers
The work to the keyboard
Has too many barriers
Don't forget about me . . .

Jane Guttman

In order to take advantage of technology, teens have to get their hands on it. Physical access is a first step in helping teens become effective users of technology. In comparison with training, this stage may seem relatively simple. But access is not a simple "yes" or "no." For the mind and hand to reach digital information you need hardware, software, a telecommunications channel, and digital files. All components need to have appropriate properties, and they must be compatible with each other. The issue of ownership versus access is also a significant factor in technology use.

HOME ACCESS

Most teens are comfortable using technology in a variety of settings: at school, home, in libraries, friends' rooms, or at Internet cafés. Teens who only have access to computers at a single location, usually at school, tend to be poorer and have parents who did not graduate from high school. Still, home access to computers and the Internet makes a significant difference in teens' technology skills and academic success, even when allowing for other variables (Wilhelm, Carmen, & Reynolds, 2002).

Although the U.S. Department of Commerce (2002) stated that in 1999 42 percent of U.S. households had personal computers and 26 percent had Internet access, only 2 percent of low-income, rural households had Internet access that same year. The good news is that since then, all sectors have shown significant increases.

- By mid-2003, 60 percent of U.S. households had computers.
- The percentage of households earning less than $15,000 per year who used the Internet increased at a 25 percent annual growth rate.
- Between 1999 and 2003, 33 percent more Blacks used the Internet and 30 percent more Latinos used the Internet.
- The percentage of rural Internet users almost equaled urban users and surpassed inner-city use, 53 percent to 54 percent.
- The West had the highest at-home and total Internet use (59.2 percent), and the South was last in at-home, outside-home, and total use, 51.6 percent.
- Renters were less likely than home owners to have a personal computer. (Compaine, 2001)

In the same study use of the Internet and computers at work was a good indicator of computer and Internet use at home; those individuals who

Figure 5.1
Internet Use at Any Location, 1998 and 2001 as a Percent of U.S. Population

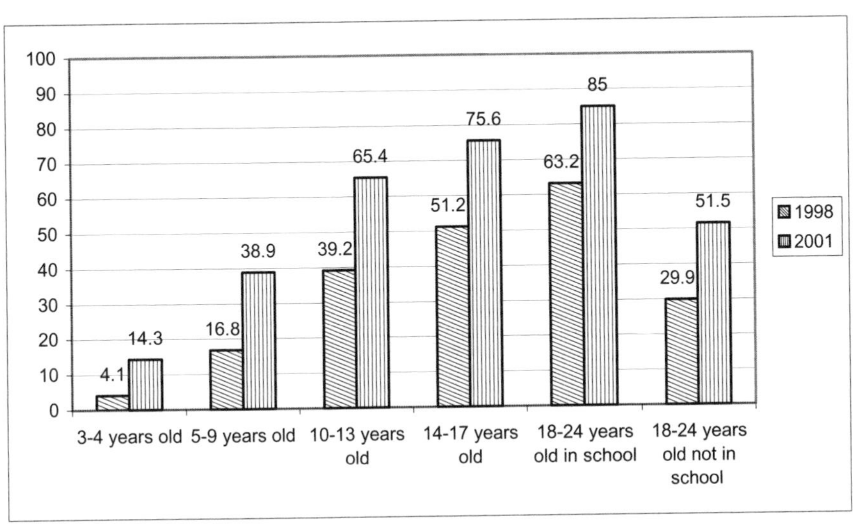

Source: NTIA and ESA, U.S. Department of Commerce, using U.S. Census Bureau Current Population Survey Supplements.

used technology at work and earned less than $15,000 per year were more likely to own a computer than a person who did not use a computer at work but made $55,000 per year (U.S. Department of Commerce, 2002, p. 64). The downside is that computer ownership remains positively correlated with income and education. In addition, poor Blacks are still less likely to have computers than poor whites.

How do these figures influence today's teens? Families with minors are more likely to have home computers (more than 70 percent) and access to the Internet (about two-thirds) than other types of families. Additionally, schools help bridge the digital divide. Fourteen to 17-year-olds make up the biggest age group of computer users. Ninety percent of youth ages 5 to 17 use computers, and 75 percent of teens ages 14 to 17 use the Internet (65 percent of 10 to 13 year olds use the Internet). How those figures apply to teens who were earlier identified as on the fringe is difficult to ascertain, but may be most easily predicted relative to ethnicity and family socioeconomics, particularly if those same youth have little disposable income.

Figure 5.2
Computer Use 1997, 2001

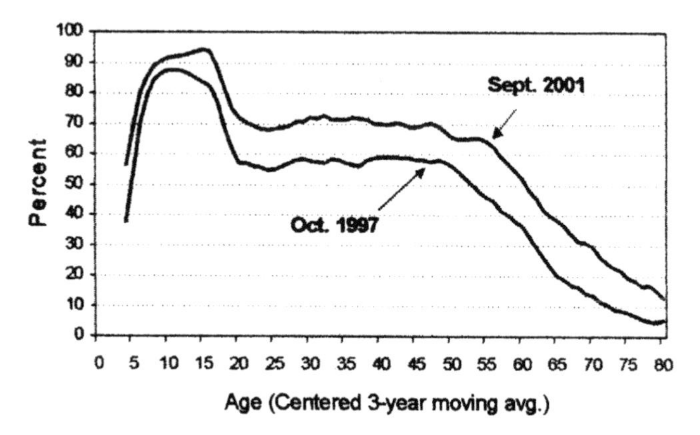

Figure 5.3
Internet Use 1997, 1998, 2000, 2001

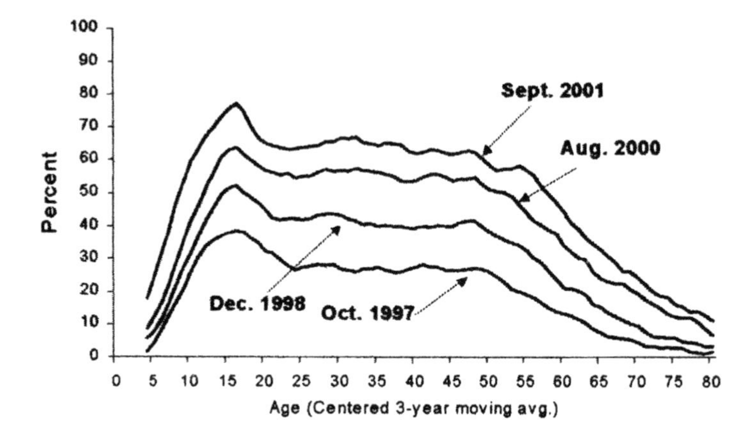

CONNECTIVITY

When applied to technology, "access" becomes a vague term. Equipment may be made available without too much difficulty, but services usually take more time and involve more complex handling. An Apple II might be adequate for simple word processing or for using an old remedial software program, but Internet access is impossible with that system. A black box that offers Internet access via television can provide access to Web sites, but productivity tools and a printer are usually absent. Thus, older systems or computer appliances such as PDAs or pocket PCs offer limited or "dedicated" functionality; they are useful, but only within specific parameters. Such equipment, including AlphaSmart (basically, a PDA that looks like a keyboard with a short "screen" area) lab packs, make the most sense in school settings where a teacher/librarian can manage their use efficiently.

In the twenty-first century, the demarcation line is Internet access; the "haves" can connect while the "have nots" cannot connect. However, even that line is fuzzy. As the Internet evolves from a text-based environment to a multimedia one, the need for broadband access becomes ever more critical. The cost for this type of connectivity can be prohibitive to individual households; public schools and libraries, however, have been given low-cost e-rates to guarantee public access to their clientele.

While major bandwidth frameworks have been established across the nation, the "last mile syndrome" remains: connecting the end commercial or agency node to the home. This issue is most prevalent in isolated rural locations and in inner cities. In both cases, public utilities and commercial enterprises have not developed a substantial technology infrastructure to support this connectivity.

Fortunately, satellite dish and wireless solutions are helping to overcome this obstacle. Two urban examples are SeattleWireless and NYCwireless. SeattleWireless is developing a citywide free wireless infrastructure for point-to-point access. NYCwireless is a volunteer organization that provides wireless Internet connectivity in public places and offers broadband Internet access in poor sections of the city. However, wireless has its own problems: interception of messages, interference from other wireless devices, and the possibility of stealing private Internet access lines.

Indeed, even if one has a computer and Internet connectivity, it does not mean that an individual has adequate access to technology. The computer might be a 286 model or a system that crashes daily. The Internet connectivity could be a 3,600 baud modem. Moreover, the Internet Service Provider (ISP) could have limited and uneven service.

The bottom line: In most cases, technology access usually implies at least a Pentium or equivalent computer system (to provide enough processing speed throughout) with at least 56K modem Internet connectivity. Fortunately, such a system can cost less than $200. However, for a family making little more than that per month, the price remains out of bounds. Even if the equipment were donated, the cost of telephone service and electricity—as well as a stable shelter—might be problematic.

In extreme cases, *access* rather than *ownership* becomes the issue. Factors that influence such access include:

- distance: access within walking distance versus the need to take public or private transportation
- stability of access point: public school or whimsical neighbor or temporary storefront
- year-round access: traditional school calendar versus public library hours
- hours of access: weekdays versus weekends; 8 AM to 3 PM school hours or 24 hours a day, 7 days a week
- length of time on a system: 15 minutes (school or library setting) versus all day
- regularity of access: one day per school semester versus daily access
- predictability: first come, first served; sign up; or random access

Since libraries constitute the number one access point for computer and Internet use among those who have no home systems (Lenhart, 2003), extra effort is needed to help fill the technology gap for those without any other access. Here are some suggestions:

- Lengthen computer-use time limits; for instance, patrons could have a weekly "bank" of time and decide for themselves how best to schedule it for maximum effectiveness.
- Let patrons sign up in advance for computer time.
- Extend hours to cover the hours when working people might be able to take advantage of access, such as staying open late a couple of nights a week or opening early on a few mornings.
- Acquire or circulate low-end systems for word processing or simple e-mail, thus reallocating computer systems according to need.
- Provide free bus "tech" passes for transportation-limited teens who join a library tech program.

Of course, all of these efforts need to be approved by library governing bodies, and usually require fiscal and staff support. The case for equitable service must be compelling.

THE OTHER ACCESS

It can be said that regardless of the equipment or the bandwidth, most Americans still do not have access to the full range of digital information.

First, not everything on the Internet is free. Although one can get *to* a site, it may cost money to access the information available at that site. Particularly because of recent court decisions about royalties paid to writers whose work appears in periodicals (*Jasini v. The New York Times*, 2001), publishers now require researchers and users to pay a fee for each article. Increasingly, online documents are accessible by subscription only. Sometimes a free and fee version of the same Web site exist simultaneously; the former gives barebones or limited information alongside advertisements and the latter provides in-depth coverage and value-added service without the ads.

Paying for the information does not guarantee its worthiness. For that reason, high-quality subscription electronic databases provide an important service. Libraries of all types are the chief purchasers of these services. At major universities, the cost can be $500,000 annually, for instance.

What do you get for that price? Information that is timely, organized, well reviewed, indexed, relevant, and easily retrievable. The subscription largely covers the costs associated with processing, storage, and legal copyright/access licenses. Not surprisingly, each company and each subscription differs in cost, coverage, and protocols. When periodical coverage largely overlaps between service providers, you need to comparison shop carefully. In terms of access, you need to ascertain how many simultaneous users can be supported, and the distance that the access can reach (especially for wifi). Furthermore, you must find out what the requirements are for accessing the information: speed, bandwidth, operating system, RAM, video, and so forth.

If you intend to allow remote access to these databases, then you should also survey your community to find out what kinds of systems are being used in local households; for instance, if most families have low-end computers that do not support Java scripting, then getting a sophisticated product might frustrate and turn off library users rather than help them.

So what about users who are limited to the "surface" Internet? They are getting less than 1 percent of the available information. At the end of 2003, almost 3.5 billion online documents had been indexed (Sullivan, 2003). By late-2004, Google was indexing over eight billion files. At the same time, almost 600 billion documents are Webconnected, 95 percent of which are publicly available (University of California, Berkeley, 2003).

The search engines used to trawl through the Internet and access information are themselves uneven in quality. Each uses a different set of algorithms, resulting in different kinds of "hits," and each has its own cache of sources. And "more" is not necessarily "better." Some search engines are limited to predefined resources, the idea being that a highly selective set of reputable Web sites is more useful than a more inclusive, uneven collection. Additionally, few producers of information use metatags to optimize retrieval, so millions of worthwhile documents may be lost because of inaccurate titles or insubstantial descriptors.

Even when access is limited to what Internet search engines can find, teens might not be able to access the information they want and need. Filtering software is now required in schools and public libraries that receive federal funding. Unfortunately, many algorithms end up banning Web sites that are appropriate and useful to students, and staff may be unfamiliar with filtering options so that they can override false limitations. Moreover, badly designed Web sites and poor networking can make access dysfunctional and electronically unstable.

In short, the road between the user and the information is long and winding and full of detours and potholes. It takes more than a computer and connectivity to access online information. In this environment, you can play a significant role as facilitators and educators. Here are some tips:

- reveal the dark Web: those sites that are not indexed through typical free search engines but may be accessed through subscription database services
- share information about library subscription databases and how to use them
- publicize and demonstrate library system in-house databases such as local information and referral systems
- create easy-to-use library Web portals with resources of interest to teens
- manually override dysfunctional filtering software algorithms so students can get needed materials for assignments
- collaborate with teachers and youth-serving agencies to offer workshops for teens on how to navigate the Internet effectively
- train teen volunteers as Net navigators and coaches

THE SCHOOL PICTURE

Often, the only place that some teens can access computer technology is at school. More than 99 percent of K-12 schools have Internet connectivity, and the ratio of instructional computers to students was 4.8 to 1 in 2002, although in poor urban schools that ratio was 5.5 to 1. Classroom access remains uneven: 79 percent of high-poverty schools have classroom Internet connections compared with 90 percent of low-poverty schools. Still, many schools have made the transition from computer labs to classroom "pods" and mobile computer carts. By 2001, the majority of schools had T1/DS1 high-speed lines, and more than 85 percent had broadband access of some sort. Schools with larger populations, high-minority rates, and located in low-income economic areas were most likely to have advanced access. In 2002, a little more than half of the schools surveyed provided computer access to students outside of school hours: 96 percent after school, 74 percent before school, 6 percent on weekends (National Center for Education Statistics, 2003a).

Nevertheless, access is uneven. On the positive side, in 83 percent of K-12 schools, the majority of teachers use technology daily for instruction or productivity, and 73 percent use the Internet for instruction. This usage is about the same for schools in high-risk areas (National Center for Education Statistics, 2003b).

However, such action does not guarantee student access. One significant reason that students are not allowed to use existing equipment is that teachers do not have good management skills to insure equitable access. Sometimes technology access is used as a reward for getting schoolwork done, with little regard to its effective use; in other cases it is used as a drill-and-kill remedial tool with little teacher diagnosis or intervention.

Gifted and talented students are often given more freedom to explore technology's outer limits, while at-risk students are not trusted with the equipment at all. Overbooked computer labs can result in uneven classroom use. In short, too often access often *follows* academic success rather then *leading* to educational achievement.

Because libraries serve a wide variety of users with a vast range of needs, they can serve as safety nets for teen access to technology. Specifically in school situations, you need to try to make sure that all students have equitable access to technology during class time, and they offer independent use time according to need before, during, and after class periods. Beyond that, you can do the following to help students get the access they need:

- provide single-sex technology training
- offer computer systems that are accessible by girls only or boys only in order to provide gender-equitable use
- proactively recruit underrepresented teens to serve as tech aides or advise with technology equity issues (i.e., high-demand digital resources, training, and so forth)
- insure that computer access is equitable through scheduling or other terms

COMMUNITY ACCESS POINTS

Increasingly, community-based institutions and coalition efforts are developing ways to expand widespread access to technology. The leaders of these organizations rightly regard such access as an investment in their own future, as residents get involved in community discussion and action. Parks and recreation centers have been typical agencies for public access, as have public housing centers. Churches and professional organizations are also getting into the picture. Even youth hostels routinely have Internet access for a dollar an hour.

Business-based portals to the public range from sections in computer stores and bookstores to Internet cafés and wifi (i.e., wireless fidelity) coffee shops. Low-cost public kiosks are appearing in shopping malls and airports. Busqueloaqui.com in Santa Ana, California, was a former storefront center where people could use and buy computers and software and also receive computer training. The owners used a membership model where, for $24.95 a month, a person could use the center's computers as long as they needed, depending on availability. Courses could be taken for additional fees. The place became a community center and had high use by Latinos because interaction was often in Spanish. Unfortunately, tight economic times caused the demise of this beneficial enterprise.

The federal government has also authorized a competitive grant process to develop community technology centers (CTC). Linked to the No Child Left Behind Act, this program seeks to facilitate technology access for underserved urban and rural areas as well as distressed communities. The Community Technology Centers' Network (http://www2.ctcnet.org/ctc/toolkit/digitaldivide.html) is a consortium of more than one thousand CTCs, which leverages government, business, and foundation support to provide money and assistance to community efforts. Their Connections for Tomorrow (C4T) project is specifically targeted to help at-risk and homeless teens. Acting as an advocacy coalition, Digitalempowerment.org links the CTC Network and other organizations to lobby Congress to insure access for all Americans.

Another popular local solution to computer access is equipment donation programs. When businesses upgrade their computer systems, they can donate their older systems to public agencies. Some computer-user clubs act as a clearinghouse for the reallocation of machines, cleaning up and reconfiguring older systems and then giving them free or at low cost to schools and other nonprofit organizations.

IBM has a program whereby teens are taught how to service computers by building them from the motherboard up; they can then take one system home for their family's use (http://www.bonita.k12.ca.us/). ThinkDetroit, a community-based program (http://www.thinkdetroit.org/leadership/computer_training.asp), also uses this approach. Communities in Schools is a national program that runs similar programs. Since home access significantly increases user competency, this approach to access is particularly attractive.

In most cases, a blend of public and private funding and technical assistance has made community access possible. As with other collaborative efforts, community access projects require detailed and broad-based planning, training, and management. Details about the steps required to develop public-private partnerships are covered in Chapter 9.

The following list highlights a few of the government and business partnership projects that provide technology to underserved populations, such as teens on the technology fringe:

- The state of Alaska and Bethel Broadcasting provided access to the Internet and to education and health services for the Yukon-Kuskokwim Delta, an isolated region populated by Native Alaskans. Building on this project the district's Web site (http://www.lksd.org) includes links to online educational resources as well as student learning activities.
- The state of California and community partners developed a community access and youth opportunity training program to help revitalize a distressed, multiethnic urban area. The resulting Eastmont Computing Center (http://www.eastmont.net) was honored by the Ford Foundation and CTCnet as one of the nations leading Community Technology Centers. Among its growing services, it now houses an Intel Computer Clubhouse that provides after school and summer programs for teens. A current proj-

ect is a College Career Team of fifty youth who will be mentored as they prepare for successful college experiences.

- The state of Michigan and the Detroit Hispanic Development Corporation offered teen gang members access to a state-of-the-art cyber café and a multimedia lab to guide them in entrepreneurial directions. By 2004, more than six thousand people have benefited from this and other programs created by this community-based corporation (http://www.dhdc1.org).
- The state of New Mexico and the University of New Mexico developed an educational computer telecommunications network to serve largely Native American and Hispanic populations. Their multicultural Web site (http://www.unm.edu/~exa10/Literary%20Links.htm) and Native American health database (http://hsc.unm.edu/library/nhd/links.cfm) exemplify their efforts to address these populations' interests and needs.
- The state of North Carolina and North Carolina Central University used a digital network in five public housing communities to link youth and their parents and grandparents by applications software, Internet browsing, and e-mail (http://topcattech.org). Through this project, an educational Web portal was developed to allow educators or organizations to create custom quizzes and tests with greater ease in order to evaluate students' skills, analyze their performance, and track progress.
- The state of Massachusetts and WGBH Educational Foundation made World Wide Web sites of public broadcasting and other organizations' Web sites accessible to individuals with visual or hearing impairments. They now provide several online options (http://ncam.wgbh.org/projects).
- The Commonwealth of Pennsylvania and United Cerebral Palsy of Central Pennsylvania provided geographically dispersed Internet computers and a virtual private network (VPN) to give persons with disabilities free access to the Internet for information, research, skill development, job search, and employment (http://www.ucp.org).

As inspiring as these community efforts are, they might not help teens access their services if they do not take into account transportation issues or hours of operation that facilitate usage of the available technology.

LIBRARIES

As previously noted, libraries often provide the only access point to technology for some teens. However, libraries may face financial constraints in acquiring the needed equipment and software. While grants and donations may temporarily help alleviate the pressure, libraries must find ongoing funding to address the subtler issue of maintenance and eventual replacement of their computer hardware and software.

An even more substantial problem faces some librarians: antiquated buildings with inadequate space or electrical power and outlets. In some cases, a wireless solution may be a better solution than rewiring an entire building. Again, funding can be an obstacle.

When setting up computer stations for teens, libraries should consider the differences between female and male teens. This issue is particularly important to young females who may feel intimidated by males "hogging" the equipment, or who desire some privacy. Additionally, some computer areas may seem unfriendly or sterile. Therefore, just as the library should create teen-friendly areas, so too should computer areas be welcoming.

Both teen and adult mothers appreciate having a children's play area near the computers so they can do online work while keeping an eye on their offspring. There should also be family stations so parents can introduce technology to their little ones; having appropriate software and bookmarked URLs lets parents concentrate on the content rather than on the time-consuming search process.

Thus, although public access to computers is a step in the right direction, also consider circulating the equipment. School librarians can work with the rest of the school community to explore the feasibility of loaning computers to families, ideally on a long-term basis. Public libraries might seek out grant funding or partnerships with other social agencies to start such a program. While universities lead the effort in circulating laptops (e.g., Regina Salve University in Rhode Island, University of California at Santa Cruz, University of Washington), public libraries (e.g., Harris County, Texas) and school libraries (e.g., Lunililo, Hawaii) also offer this service.

Several types of options exist for loan programs: older or refurbished desktop systems, low-end laptops, Internet "in a box" (e.g., MSN TV) that connect to family televisions and telephone lines, Internet add-ons for video game systems, and handheld computers. It appears that Internet connectivity is a key consideration when choosing systems. Also, as textbooks on CD-ROMs become more prevalent, schools must ensure that the equipment can handle that format, adding an external drive if needed. In fact, Forney Independent School District (Texas) is making the transition from textbooks to digital resources; each fifth and sixth grader receives a laptop loaded with the curriculum's textbooks and 2,000 public domain documents (Ishizuka, 2004).

Of course, circulating the equipment has its perils. Even within school settings where clear and stringent policies can be enforced, issues about responsibility for theft, loss, and destruction must be carefully considered and addressed. For instance, the youngster who is reluctant to borrow a book for fear of losing it is not a good candidate for borrowing a computer. Transient families may not be good risks for long-term loans. Additionally, equipment may be returned in an altered or dysfunctional state, which takes valuable (and scarce) staff time to fix. Sometimes the easiest approach is for libraries, in collaboration with local companies, to train families on how to use and maintain a computer, and then give them a system donated by a local entity. Two successful community-based recycled computer programs are Computers for Schools and eTrek (Minkel, 2004). Another approach is to work with small community businesses that might have a public access corner where teens could use a donated computer system on a sign-up or low-cost basis.

SPECIAL ACCESS ISSUES FOR PEOPLE WITH DISABILITIES

Even as access in the community and in libraries looks promising, one group stands out on the losing side. Only 40 percent of people with disabilities use the Internet, as opposed to 75 percent by nondisabled individuals. In most public places where technology access is provided, assistive technology is largely absent; ironically, some people with disabilities do not have the transport to get to these public locations in the first place. It should also be noted that the primary reason that students with disabilities do not use computers is because many teachers do not know how to use them themselves or are unable to use them as instructional tools, particularly in alignment with Individualized Education Plans (IEP) (Greene & Kochhar-Bryant, 2003).

The Charlotte (NC) Public Library's Virtual Village Communication Center demonstrates the strong belief in technology for *all* users, and focuses on individuals with disabilities. This is a model that more libraries should emulate. Assistive technology ranges from scanners to Braille embossers, from voice-recognition software to Cyberlink headbands. A Digital Darkroom enables patrons to transfer, edit, and publish images. Videos can be produced, and a Video Relay Service enables hard-of-hearing patrons to communicate through a signing interpreter. MIDI (Musical Instrument Digital Interface) keyboards facilitate digital compositions. Even "hackable" stations are available to explore. Instruction is available through classes, videotapes, and individualized computer instruction (Peasley, 2002). Funding for this long-term commitment comes from successful library bond issues, numerous grants, business donations, community fund-raising campaigns, and broad-based county support. Even little touches make a difference: a link on the library's Web portal to Amazon.com enables users to buy books for the library on the spot.

For a significant portion of the disabled teenage population, no matter the bandwidth or the number of computers available, access to technology is still problematic. The reason? Lack of universal design and accommodations, particularly as they apply to the needs of people with physical differences. Modifications can be as simple as adjusting a table so that a wheelchair can slide underneath or enlarging the text size on the screen or adding sophisticated assistive technology such as specialized headgear to trigger key responses. Families should not have to supply their teens with these adaptive technologies, but special education facilities are often underfunded in this area.

Assistive technology is usually the first consideration in providing accommodation for physical access. It may be defined as "any item, piece of equipment, or product system that is used to increase, maintain or improve functional capabilities of a child with a disability" (Individuals with Disabilities Education Act, Public Law 101-476).

As a librarian, you can start by dealing with the teen first: his or her capabilities and needs, then the task at hand. As you consider a strategy, be sensitive to the teen's motivation as well as the social context. Other factors include training and support, durability and portability, and the simplicity of your solution. The following list of physical differences and supportive assistive technology provides a starting point so that you can optimize physical access:

- visual differences: larger text size on monitors, change in screen background design and color, reading software (including Mac's SimpleText and Windows Narrative), scanners, oral-input devices
- hearing differences: closed-captioned materials, transcriptions, amplification devices

- mobility differences: seating options, trackballs and joysticks, digital controls (e.g., switches and scanning), oral-input devices

If and when you decide to buy assistive technology, a comprehensive list of major distributors can be found at http://www.abledata.com/Site_2/assistiv.htm.

The concept of universal design is that products and environments can be designed so that all people can use them without modification. Thus, a text-only Web site without frames that is easy to navigate and uses simple language would be accessible by most people. A simple Web site is also easier to load, making it a less frustrating experience for teens with low-end Internet access. Some of the basic principles of universal design include simplicity, flexibility, intuitive use, tolerance of error (compensating for unintended or accidental actions), and low physical effort (Center for Universal Design, 1997).

With the passage of new government and industry guidelines regulating Web accessibility for users with disabilities, librarians are required to comply with Section 508 of the Rehabilitation Act of 1973 (http://www.section508.gov) and priority one standards of the World Wide Web Consortium's Web Content Accessibility Guidelines (http://www.w3.org/WAI). In substance, to create accessible Web sites, the following points need to be incorporated:

- caption or use the ALT attribute to describe images and functions
- summarize or use a LONGDESC attribute for graphs and charts
- make tables readable line by line
- label hyperlinks (avoid "click here")
- have a consistent layout
- avoid frames, provide alternatives to pdf formatted documents
- provide alternative content if applets or plug-ins are not supported by reader software

Universal design in Web page development also applies to English language learners and illiterate populations. Thus, a variety of formats and sensory modes should be available: sound for illiterates, images for those teens who have difficulty reading English, translations for those who read another language. Consider having more than one version of a Web site to accommodate those differences; asking teens to help develop these variations can be a real service—and a valuable experience for them.

The Association of Specialized and Cooperative Library Agencies initiative on equity of access provides some good tips for obtaining e-rate discounts, providing broadband Internet access, insuring universal service, and dealing with federal regulations such as filtering (http://www.ala.org/ASCLATemplate.cfm?Section=Issues). Other sites that are particularly helpful include:

- About.Com-Special Education: http://specialed.about.com/mbody.htm
- Ability Hub: Assistive Technology Solutions: http://www.abilityhub.com/
- Alliance for Technology Access: http://www.ataccess.org
- Assistive Technology Act Projects: http://www.resna.org/taproject/at/statecontacts.html
- Association of Specialist and Cooperative Library Agencies Initiative on Equity of Access: http://www.ala.org/ascla/issues.html#access
- Center for Applied Special Technology: http://www.cast.org
- ERIC Clearinghouse on Disabilities and Gifted Education: http://www.ericec.org
- Equal Access for Software and Information: http://www.rit.edu/~easi
- Federal Access Board: http://www.access-board.gov
- Internet Resources for Special Children: http://www.irsc.org
- National Center of Dissemination of Disability Research: http://www.ncddr.org
- National Rehabilitation Information Center: http://www.naric.com
- Recordings for the Blind and Dyslexic: http://www.rfbd.org
- SERI: Special Education Resources on the Internet: http://seriweb.com/
- World Wide Web Consortium's Web Content Accessibility Guidelines: http://www.w3.org/WAI

SUPPORTING WEB SITES

The following Web sites provide information on developing physical access to technology for fringe teens. Most of the programs are a result of community-based efforts. Several deal explicitly with digital divide issues. You can find out what works in your library—and what does not—so your projects will be more likely to succeed.

City Strategy for Youth Services
http://www.city.richmond.bc.ca/youth/strategy/youth_rep99.htm
Richmond (Canada) community-wide plan for reaching and serving youth.

Community Technology Centers
http://www.ed.gov/programs/comtechcenters/index.html
U.S. Department of Education model programs providing technology access to youth and adults.

Community Technology Centers' Network
http//www.ctcnet.org
How to plan and implement community technology centers.

Community Technology Resources
http://www.jointventure.org
Silicon Valley Network of local technology resources to address the digital divide.

Digital Divide Solutions
http://www.asu.edu/DigitalDivideSolutions
Programs, resources, funding, research, and policies collected through the partnership of Arizona State University's Hispanic Research Center and the College Board.

Digital Equity Toolkit
http://www.nici-nc2.org/de_toolkit/pages/toolkit.htm
Tips from the National Institute for Community Innovations on ways to get free and inexpensive resources to help bridge the digital divide (e.g., ISP, Web page hosting, computers).

Do It!
www.washington.edu/doit/Faculty
Disabilities, Opportunities, Internetworking, and Technology.

Neighborhood Networks
http://www.hud.gov/nnw/nnwpubs.htm
U.S. Department of Housing and Urban Development guidance on neighborhood networks.

Public Space in Cyberspace
http://www.lff.org/programs/community.html
Public library community-based technology programs.

Today's teenagers will find computer access somehow if they want to (Murray, 2004). However, today, libraries serve as a societal safety net for physical access to technology, particularly to online information. As librarians, you can build on that positive reputation and confirm its validity as you work with teens and insure responsible oversight and guidance. By assessing community technology access points and identifying key decision makers and financial backers, you can maximize technology access through effective partnerships. Investing in young people through technology access makes good sense.

WORKS CITED

Center for Universal Design. (1997). *What is universal design?* Raleigh, NC: North Carolina State University. http://www.design.ncsu.edu/cud/univ_design/princ_overview.htm.

Compaine, B. (Ed.) (2001). *The digital divide: Facing a crisis or creating a myth?* Cambridge, MA: MIT Press.

Greene, G., & Kochhar-Bryant, C. (2003). *Pathways to successful transition for youth with disabilities.* Upper Saddle River, NJ: Merrill.

Ishizuka, K. (2004, July). A Texas district goes digital. *School Library Journal, 50*(7), 14.

Lenhart, A. (2003). *The ever-shifting Internet population: A new look at Internet access and the digital divide.* Washington, DC: The Pew Internet and American Life Project. http://www.pewinternet.org/pdfs/PIP_Shifting_Net_Pop_Report.pdf.

Minkel, W. (2004, July). As good as new: Recycled computers are a boon to cash-strapped schools. *School Library Journal, 50*(7), 27.

Murray, C. (2004, April). Students see tech as necessity, say schools fall short. *eSchool News,* 26.

National Center for Education Statistics. (2003a). *Internet access in U.S. public schools and classrooms: 1994–2001.* Washington, DC: National Center for Education Statistics.

National Center for Education Statistics. (2003b). *School and staff survey, 1999–2000.* Washington, DC: National Center for Education Statistics.

Peasley, B. (2002, June). It takes a virtual village to empower all the villagers. *American Libraries, 33*(6), 54–56.

Sullivan, D. (2003, September 2). Search engine size. SearchEngineWatch.com. http://www.searchenginewatch.com/reports/sizes.html.

University of California, Berkeley. School of Information Management and Systems. (2003). *How much information?* Berkeley, CA: University of California, Berkeley. http://www.sims.berkeley.edu/research/projects/how-much-info-2003/.

U.S. Department of Commerce. (2002). *A nation online: How Americans are expanding their use of the Internet.* Washington, DC: U.S. Department of Commerce. http://www.ntia.doc.gov/ntiahome/dn/.

Wilhelm, T., Carmen, D., & Reynolds, M. (2002). *Connecting kids to technology: Challenges and opportunities.* Baltimore, MD: Annie E. Casey Foundation. http://www.aypf.org/forumbriefs/2002/fb071802.htm.

6

TECHNICAL ACCESS TO TECHNOLOGY

Digit. Dig it?

"It's all Greek" to those fringers . . .
Invite them to mess around
with their digital fingers.
The only fingerin' that's goin' down
is to the Man.
That's a language I understand.

Lesley Farmer and Jane Guttman

It is not enough to have the equipment and the connectivity if the user cannot turn on the computer, log on, search for, or save information. Each of those tasks requires a skill. The group of skills described above is a skill set, just one of a number of competencies needed in order to make sense of digital information and use it. To use a language analogy, if the directions are in Greek, and the user reads only English—or is illiterate—no matter how much text there is, it's "all Greek" to the user, and just as useless.

Several entities have noted the importance of technical competency for its own sake. The 1991 Secretary's Commission on Achieving Necessary

Skills, or SCANS report listed technology skills as one of the five major competencies that future employees should exhibit. The CEO Forum (2001), a coalition of businesses and organizations, produced yearly reports on students and technology. They asserted that technology could improve student academic achievement and help them develop twenty-first century skills, and that young people should also become digitally competent. The U.S. Department of Education has taken those recommendations to heart, particularly for noncollege-bound students (Teitelbaum & Kaufman, 2002).

Therefore, even before thinking about content or use, consider how you can make sure that teens on the digital fringes are able to operate technology sufficiently well to perform the tasks they want to do—or achieve things that will be worthwhile for them. To that end, you need to motivate teens to take the first step to learning, and you need to provide effective venues for learning and practicing those skills in meaningful activities.

WHAT IS THERE TO LEARN?

The first thing any computer user must learn in order to gain access to technology is basic operating skills—in other words, mechanical access. This skill typically involves the following tasks:

1. input and output: mouse and keyboarding, printer use
2. file management
3. word processing
4. using a Web browser and moving between programs

In addition, users should be able to perform basic operations such as troubleshooting normal problems (e.g., inability to print, get Internet access, open and close an application).

Of course, additional skills help teens manipulate data and information in order to interpret and organize them in efficient and effective ways. The standard technology productivity applications are databases, spreadsheets, and presentation programs. At this point, basic computer operations also entail telecommunications skills: e-mail, attachments, and file transfer. Basic training should also include technology consumerism: how to "spec" a system and peripherals (i.e., specifying the features needed) so that when teens get into a position to acquire technology, for themselves or their employers, they can communicate knowledgeably and make reasoned decisions. In today's world, teens also need to learn how to be safe and polite on the Internet.

HOW DO TEENS LEARN TO USE TECHNOLOGY?

Many teachers or other adults automatically assume that all young people can handle technology. When adults look at the number of hours that youth spend on video games, they assume that these youngsters are technologically competent. This is not the case; a different skill set is needed to play FPS (first-person-shooters) games than to surf the Net for information.

How do teens usually learn how to navigate the Internet and use technology? They "mess around" on computers—they explore, they take risks. At school they learn the formal, official skills. All due and proper. But, sadly, such training seldom connects with their personal interests or needs.

Additionally, because of school strictures on e-mail and chat, filtering software for the Internet, downloading constraints against piracy, and system programming (e.g., directory management, configuration, system controls), the very skills that attract teens to using technology are prohibited. It must be noted that many of these same parameters exist in library settings, so as you encourage teens to use your library, you will have to develop clear policies and communicate your expectations in order to avoid conflict and frustration on both sides.

Of course, hands-on learning is the most effective for teens. Because of strong social interests, instruction should provide opportunities for peer collaboration, as well as chances for individual work for those teens who prefer to work alone. A teen techno-buddy is probably preferable to an adult coach. As with adults, teens prefer just-in-time learning: what they need to learn when they need to learn it. Because teens usually do not need as much help as adults in getting comfortable with technology, training can usually concentrate on getting started with the basics and then letting them explore on their own. However, teens need very clear directions; one-page guide sheets at the relevant computer stations are useful, particularly if they include screen "dumps" (printouts of the screen images) and other visual cues.

Remember that teens will advance more quickly if they can practice their skills frequently. Consider the fact that teens often avoid phone help because they become frustrated by waiting for long periods of time for overworked online tech help. They may also feel that they sound too young on the phone and will therefore get poor service.

How do you overcome some of these obstacles to learning? In most cases, the solution is to address the problem as soon as possible (e.g., fix machines that crash, get tech support, use visual cues or learning buddies for ELL). Following is a summary of the problems that can arise.

- mechanics: unstable machines and sudden equipment problems, system freezes and crashes, viruses, slow speed, insufficient RAM, narrow bandwidth
- Internet issues: changing URLs, changing navigation methods, "locked" sites, cookies, unreadable files (e.g., non-Roman alphabet, frames that reader software cannot overcome)
- legalities and security: actions counter to acceptable use policies (e.g., accessing inappropriate Web sites, downloading copyrighted materials, piracy), filtering, "lost" student cards needed to use equipment
- lack of tech support: lack of self-knowledge about troubleshooting, constraints on being able to fix problems (e.g., adults usually will not let teens reprogram or reinstall software)
- time: sessions long enough to learn and practice a skill; schedule follow-up sessions close enough and often enough for teens to remember the training and internalize the procedures
- lack of context: teens do not know why they are learning a skill (e.g., creating a database)
- lack of typing/keyboarding skills
- physical differences or limitations (e.g., motor control, attention deficit, visual impairment): assistive technology and other accommodations needed to address individual needs
- illiteracy or lack of English fluency: accommodations may include learning buddies, visual cues, simple language, sites in other languages
- psychological/emotional issues: teenage males may feel uncomfortable if they do not already know how to use technology; girls may perceive technology as a "guy" thing and devalue it—or make fun of girl techies; families may feel threatened by tech-savvy teens

- motivation: teens may not see the benefit of technology training; they may have had negative experiences in this area and might be unwilling learners because of personal issues

Fortunately, training can be done in several ways to accommodate teens with different learning skills. For instance, deaf teens can read and watch instruction, illiterate teens can listen and watch, English language learners can watch demonstrations and look at visual cues and diagrams. Much of the basic computer operation consists of watching an expert (or knowledgeable user) perform an action and then mimicking that process. And if the instructor models the desired action well, incorporates meaningful content and learning activities, coaches students as needed, and addresses their emotional needs, then the psychological barriers usually come down. The tougher skill is intellectual access, which is discussed in Chapter 7.

INSTRUCTIONAL ISSUES

Basic computer skills are introduced increasingly early in formal education. If the equipment is available, teachers and librarians help students operate systems even in kindergarten. In many instances, the chief stumbling block to learning may be adults who lack technological knowledge and skills.

This can be a tricky issue because such a wide range of approaches to the problem exist. Some educators just tell students to "go on the Net" and explore for themselves, using the laissez-faire or trial-and-error method, which is neither efficient nor pedagogically sound. On the other hand, others are fearful of letting young people touch the computer until "the adult in charge" knows all the details of the application to be used.

In the case of getting teens comfortable with technology so they can take advantage of it, educators likely know enough to get them started on whatever application is being used, particularly if the objective is accessing and manipulating subject content matter. When technical questions arise, emphasis should be placed on showing teens how to get assistance through help screens, guide sheets and manuals, and Web FAQs. Thus, you can help teens learn how to identify relevant key words, how to ask the right questions, and how to take notes and follow directions. These skills should be part of the knowledge base of most educators, even if they are tech neophytes.

Engagement is another key to technical learning and competency. Again, traditional classroom management and instruction come into play. Some of the basic practices used in teaching technology include:

- giving teens choices: content, search engines, and so on
- using programs and activities that encourage interactivity
- taking advantage of technology's various formats to vary instruction and learning
- breaking down the activity into manageable parts at which teens can succeed; this approach also helps pace instruction for a large group, so no one gets hopelessly behind and quick learners can help their peers
- encouraging responsibility for self-learning
- providing immediate feedback
- emphasizing effort rather than mastery
- keeping a sense of humor
- remaining flexible, and ready to use plan B

As implied above, the format of the content and the communications channel has an impact on engaged learning. Because technology combines text, visuals, and sound, students with different learning styles can be accommodated effectively. Particularly in informal educational settings such as libraries, teens should be able to choose how they want to learn along several dimensions:

- content: word processing, desktop management, e-mail, Internet navigation, and so forth
- scope of information: overview, main concepts and skills, single technique
- objective: introduction, basics, advanced skills, review
- grouping: individually, pairs, small group, class
- timeframe: anywhere from one minute to one day, as well as a series of days
- method: demonstration, hands-on instruction, video presentation, multimedia presentation, Web tutorial, guide sheets, handbook
- instructor: librarian, technician, adult, peer, online expert

Because technologically underserved teens may be reluctant to endure formal training or may have experienced negative educational experiences or may not feel comfortable with peers who have different levels of technological expertise, offering training sessions to this population is not always easy. Some tips include:

- advertising and locating training periods to attract a narrow spectrum of teens (i.e., pregnant teens, Latino dropouts, visually impaired, and so on)
- facilitating training where participants are at the same level of competence
- offering training as part of the efforts of an audience-focused public agency (e.g., sports group, Goodwill, housing project, and so forth)
- setting up peer coaching or low trainer-to-trainee ratios with older teens as the trainers
- weaving in training as a means to an end, such as owning a computer (by learning how to put one together) or broadcasting original hip hop (by learning how to use MIDI systems and developing streaming video and Web pages)
- combining social and technical activities
- providing a series of module trainings (1 to 3 sessions) so teens can enter at several points, but also have an opportunity for sustained engagement

Libraries are ideal learning environments for technology because they offer a variety of resources within flexible parameters. The key is to let teenagers know what is available and under what conditions. With this specialization approach not all teens will be learning the same thing, but what learning does take place will be more suited to teens' needs and incorporated more quickly. Thus, teens need to know up front what is acceptable behavior, how much the staff can help them, and to what extent other people need to use the same resources. Signs, flyers, desktop screen saver messages, and personal contact are all ways to communicate those messages so teens can feel comfortable in the library.

As with other ethical issues, you can assume a leadership role in helping teens practice safe, legal, and moral behavior using technology. Intellectual property is even more important—and complex—in the

Internet world. The safety and well-being of teenagers can be problematic in cyberspace, particularly in chat rooms. Etiquette still matters in tech environments. As a librarian you, more than any other adult, understand the issues and can explore them with teens in a proactive manner. While many school libraries do not encourage telecommunications for a variety of reasons (e.g., filtering software, supervision problems, accountability if a student is solicited online, flaming [i.e., insulting] incidents, and so forth), you can still help teens understand how to converse safely online. Below are some sites that have good information on Internet safety.

- Cybersmart Kids (http://www.cybersmartkids.com)
- Safeteens.com (http://safekids.com/safeteens)
- Kids' Rules for Online Safety (http://safekids.com/kidsrules.htm)
- Core Rules of Netiquette (http://www.albion.com/netiquette/corerules.html)
- Online Safety for Kids and Teens (http://www.wiredkids.org)
- Promoting Online Safety: The Home-School Partnership (http://safewiredschools.cosn.org/toolkit/files.cfm)

VENUES FOR LEARNING

While schools constitute the standard location for formal technology training, they certainly are not the only venue, and not all teens attend school. As noted earlier, home use vies for the top spot in boosting technical learning if for no other reason than young people have more opportunity to explore their own interests and control their learning at home. On the negative side, if parents are not tech-savvy, they will not be able to help their children learn as efficiently. Home use must encompass access to relatives' and friends' home systems as well. As noted in Chapter 5, public places such as libraries, recreation centers, housing complexes, Internet cafés, computer stores, and churches can be sites for learning. The key to success is instruction.

Basic technology training is usually not considered a core function of the library. Instead, librarians like to focus on intellectual access to the ever-widening world of information. However, your library can collaborate with individuals and groups to facilitate just-in-time learning.

Referral Services

The easiest approach is training referral services. You can develop databases of local entities that provide free and low-cost training. That information can be posted in the library as well as on the library's Web portal, and flyers can be disseminated in local public places where teens naturally congregate. Of course, you should investigate the quality of these services, and get their permission to publicize them before making a recommendation. This effort is actually a good public service and benefits all parties. For example, the Multnomah County (Oregon) Library has a good links page on technology and games for teens (http://www.multcolib.org/outer/techgames.html) and the McMillan Memorial Library (Wisconsin Rapids) lists Web tutorials and local technology classes (http://www.scls.lib.wi.us/mcm/ref/internet_computer.html).

Training at the Library

If your library has a bank of computers and general low-use times, then a simple solution is to have technology experts do training sessions, preferably pro bono. Trainers might come from:

- local businesses that have volunteer programs in place
- retired professionals
- computer user-group members
- teen technology groups

Note that tech-savvy teens might not know how to teach others so you should get in touch with the adult advisor to discuss training needs and parameters.

If adults and teens work together to develop appropriate training approaches, that activity itself becomes a positive learning experience and helps teens gain vocational expertise. Some examples of libraries that offer technology training include the Carnegie Library of Pittsburgh PC Center, which offers regular training workshops; the Springfield-Greene County (Missouri) Library System, which offers technology workshops and other tech-enhanced classes (e.g., SAT preparation) for teens and the general public; the St. Charles (Illinois) Public Library, which has a tech center that is available for group instruction and individual use; are the

Bettendorf (Iowa) Public Library, which uses teens as tech trainers. As well, Providence (Rhode Island) hires teen tech trainers.

Partnerships

A number of other partnerships between educational institutions and community entities have effective programs in place to reach teens and help them learn technical skills. Consider having your library join in these partnerships to support technology training, particularly for teens on the fringe. Following is a sample of success stories.

- Black Data Processing Associates (Cincinnati, OH) has partnered with sixteen entities to provide technology training for African Americans through tech camps. Graduates become tech trainers in their own right (http://www.bdpa-cincy.org).
- The Bronx (New York) Educational Opportunity Center targets inner-city youth and adults, providing technology training and involving them in community-based tech projects (http://www.uwnyc.org/technews/training.html).
- Kidz Online, a multimedia-based endeavor led by a consortium of educational and business groups that works with local teens to produce Web-enhanced and multimedia technology training (http://www.kidzonline.org).
- MOUSE (Making Opportunities for Upgrading Schools and Education) is a nonprofit effort with New York City schools to train inner-city teens in technology and have them in turn develop tech help desks for their schools (http://www.mouse.org).
- The Puget Sound (Washington) Center for Teaching, Learning and Technology represents a coalition of educational, business, governmental, and private foundation providers. Their training program, TechReach, targets low-income, at-risk middle school girls (http://www.pugetsoundcenter.org/ddivide/ditg.html).

Online Training

The following Web sites offer free and low-cost online instruction. Computer companies and technology publishing sites often include tutorials, which are another good set of sources to use. At the very least, you can set up a training page within your Web portal to help direct teens to self-learning options.

Find Tutorials
http://www.findtutorials.com
Contains hundreds of free Web-based tutorials on technology.

Free Skills
http://www.freeskills.com
Free online tutorials for technology skills are found on this Web site.

Go4IT
http://www.go4it.gov
A U.S. Department of Commerce Web site with information on hundreds of Information Technology (IT) education, employment, and training programs, with an opportunity for schools to submit their own programs for listing on the Web site.

Goodwill Global Learning
http://www.gcflearnfree.org/en/main/community.asp
Provides online and class training on job searching, work skills, and computer skills.

Learn the Net
http://www.Learnthenet.com/English/index.html
Commercial site with low-tech and high-tech tutorials; available in Spanish, French, German, and Italian.

PowerUp
http://www.powerup.org
Resources and programs to help young people learn computer skills.

Spider's Apprentice: A Helpful Guide to Web Search Engines
http://www.monash.com/spidap.html
Explains how leading search engines work.

Tech4Learning
http://www.tech4learning.com/
Tech lessons and other resources, including multimedia skills, are on this site.

Typing Practice
http://www.gwydir.demon.co.uk/jo/learn/typing.htm
Fun format and timed competitions for learning how to type.

YouthLearn
http://www.youthlearn.org/techno/hardware.asp
A crash course in devices for your lab.

The bottom line? Teens need to feel comfortable with technology before they can take advantage of its benefits. Libraries are prime locales that offer a variety of methods and flexible schedules to accommodate individual needs and capacities. As you get to know your clientele and develop trusting relationships with them, you can provide optimum learning activities that meet teen needs as well as allocate library resources and services in a cost-effective manner.

WORKS CITED

CEO Forum on Education and Technology. (2001). *School technology and readiness report: Year 4 report.* Washington, DC: CEO Forum on Education and Technology. http://www.ceoforum.org/downloads/report4.pdf.

Secretary's Commission on Achieving Necessary Skills. (1991). *What work requires of schools: A SCANS report for America 2000.* Washington, DC: Department of Labor.

Teitelbaum, P., & Kaufman, P. (2002). *Labor Market Outcomes of Non-College-Bound High School Graduates.* Washington, DC: U.S. Department of Education (NCES 2002–126).

7

INTELLECTUAL ACCESS TO TECHNOLOGY

Step out of poverty
Step out of drugs
Step out of unemployment
Step out of illiteracy
Step out of crime
Step out of shame
Step out of despair
Information literacy is the ladder to life

Jane Guttman

Many teens consider themselves tech-savvy, and most can certainly find their way around the Internet. However, critical evaluation skills are often overlooked in these assertions or assumed to be unnecessary, much to the distress of librarians who witness teens using the first entry of a Google "hit" regardless of its worthiness or relevance. Teens too often overlook valuable information in favor of easy hits, in a similar fashion to those teens who use only a general encyclopedia for every research project. In addition, teens might not understand what they are accessing: authorship, perspective, or underlying message. Even when teens find the information they want, they might not know what to do with it. These skills come under the umbrella of "information literacy," which is a vital skill if teens are to benefit from technology.

When dealing with "tech-not" teens, you need to address an additional layer of intellectual understanding. You must be sensitive to the different ways that young adults learn, cultural or physiological. Although the picture is changing as the Internet offers increased intellectual access through sight and sound, for the illiterate, the Internet has not really delivered in this area. New Americans, in particular, can feel stymied by the overpowering presence of English-language electronic sources. When primary languages use non-Roman alphabets or other written systems, the barriers go up dramatically. Sometimes even images are insufficient for understanding if their meaning or connotations bear no relationship to teens' prior experiences.

THE TECHNOLOGY WORLD

The world of digital information has become increasingly large and complex, particularly on the World Wide Web. What started as a sequential textual environment added another dimension through hypertext, has now come to embrace multimedia and incorporates interactive components that appear to change content in response to user responses.

Other formats for digital information have also been transformed over the past decade. CD-ROMs still have their place for stable storage, but DVDs have replaced them in order to store large amounts of sound and visuals. Additionally, DVDs typically include menu and search features that allow greater flexibility in access and use.

Handheld computers and cell phones have increased utility through Internet accessibility. They also allow for peer-to-peer transfer of information. While few libraries deal with these personal devices, they may well portend another service-sector option for libraries, with a more acceptable format than the clunky e-book readers that never got off the ground.

INFORMATION LITERACY

At its most profound level, literacy enables you to connect with the world in terms of constructing meaning as well as acting on it. Information literacy specifically deals with the skills that enable you to locate, evaluate, select, use, and share information effectively. While that skill set also applies to nontechnology settings, this section focuses on teaching and learning information literacy competencies within the technology environment.

Keep in mind that you can help teens make sense of information and the research process through "translating" steps across disciplines. Developing a hypothesis relates to developing a thesis statement. Numerical analysis methods can be used in science and social studies, and interpretation applies to music as well as to poetry (Farmer, 2001). If teens feel self-confident in one area, they have the logical capacity to transfer those skills to another subject. Information literacy thus acts as a lingua franca.

When technology is used across disciplines as well, then teens have an additional opportunity to make connections and find meaning in the information they seek. Thus, you should familiarize yourself with your local school curriculum in order to align your information instruction to those content areas and related standards as a way to optimize learning. Obviously, school librarians have greater opportunities to work with the school community toward that end, but public librarians can also work with school staff as well in support of teens' academic needs. Moreover, all librarians can show teens that these competencies apply to the real world and can serve them well throughout their lives.

Locating Information

Locating information remains a core library function. Now, however, it transcends finding a book on the shelf or getting a magazine article, to developing a search strategy to access the most relevant and developmentally appropriate resources—in the most appropriate media—in a timely manner for the purpose at hand. Several substeps are required to accomplish this: identify the task, determine what information is needed, and figure out the best way to find that information.

In school settings, even at middle and high school levels, assignments are usually defined by the teachers. As such, teens do not get enough opportunities to self-identify a task and link it to information literacy skills. While teens may well identify their problems in life, such as dealing with divorce or finding a job, they might not see the connection between those life issues and school research projects—or technology.

As a librarian, you can help bridge that intellectual gap by showing teens digital resources that deal with those problems. And if those issues are discussed and resolved to teens' satisfaction, they may develop an awareness that technology can help them on a personal level.

Assessment

In terms of determining what information is needed, graphic organizers come in handy to help teens analyze the task. School librarians are most likely to help teens with this step, although public librarians often facilitate this process through reference interviews. Online reference services also explicitly deal with identifying information needs; if the interaction is archived, teens can retrace the thinking process and use it for another problem. Another approach is to "cluster" or "parse" possible concepts into categories.

Two search engines lend themselves particularly well to this exercise. Vivisimo (http://www.vivisimo.com) clusters Web sites about a topic or phrase. For instance, if you type in "teen parenting," the search engine lists URLs on pregnancy, parenting, teen moms, and teen parents groups.

Kartoo (http://www.kartoo.com) generates a concept map, lists topics, and links major Web sites. If you type in "car purchase," this search engine lists the following topics: vehicle purchase, dealers, lease, price quotes, finance, obligations, and buying advice. Furthermore, the user can click on specific aspects or linked factors, and generate another map. In either case, teens can narrow their information focus.

Searching for Information

Once teens determine what kind of information to find, they need to figure out where it can be found. Technology offers a rich platter of options: videos, audiocassettes, CDs, DVDs, online subscription databases, and Web sites. Ideally, your library should provide information in these media. Concurrently, the library's catalog should list resources in different formats so teens do not have to look in a number of different indexes or lists. While the first consideration is subject matter, the second factor could well be the medium, particularly for teens on the fringe.

For example, a video could be a good choice for illiterates or English language learners if the images can tell the needed story. An audio recording of a drama could help the visually impaired or the dyslexic. Mass media resources can be useful for late-breaking news. Subscription databases may be the best choice for age-appropriate, readable, high-quality information to meet a required class assignment. You can also mention that good information can be found by asking experts, although care should be taken to check the credentials of people online. Web sites, in general, range so widely that careful evaluation is usually needed to determine their usefulness and verity. In any case, you can help teens determine where to begin, and also encourage them to use a variety of resources if you do not have all the needed information.

Evaluating and Selecting Information

In the print world of the traditional library, the user had only to determine if a resource was useful and appropriate vis-à-vis readability and maturity level of information. True, the point of view was important to establish the author's agenda and its fit with the user's purpose, but one usually did not have to worry that the author was nefarious or totally outrageous. The main reason for this was that the librarian carefully chose each resource.

In the digital world, all bets are off. Librarians cannot control what Internet sites flow in, even with the assistance of filtering software. Still, some teenagers, particularly the technologically naïve, may believe that everything on the Internet is credible. Some parents, on the other hand, fear that pornography reigns in cyberspace and that all information on the Net is false. Both extreme attitudes need to be addressed through education.

Certainly you can bookmark relevant Web sites and develop subject Webliographies. You also need to encourage teens to use subscription electronic databases of indexed, high-quality sources that meet curricular needs. These practices help teens understand what a good site looks like and how it operates. Such lists, however, do not help teenagers become self-sufficient information evaluators, which is a necessary lifelong skill.

Therefore, show teens Web sites that have questionable content, and teach them how to differentiate between the two. For instance, The Good, the Bad, and the Ugly (http://lib.nmsu.edu/instruction/eval.html) provides criteria, examples, and suggested activities. Give teens the tools to evaluate information independently as much as you can; this approach builds independence and reflects your belief in their critical skills.

Having a one-page list of criteria by Internet-connected systems can also provide subtle instruction for teens who might be reluctant to ask for help. QUICK: the Quality Information Checklist (http://www.quick.org.uk/menu.htm) is a teen-friendly, one-page summary of evaluation criteria questions. Of course, you need to be sensitive to the cultural values and experiences of immigrant teens, in particular, who are taught not to question authority or think independently.

While you can assist teenagers on an individual basis to critique potential resources, the time required to do a good job limits the number of people that you can reach. So take advantage of other Net-savvy people to help train library users. Remember, enlisting the help of teens increases the library's credibility and reputation among youth.

As with other jobs, potential technology aides need to be interviewed and assessed in terms of their technology competency and people skills. The Web surfer may still need to be trained in subtle evaluation skills and may need to be introduced to subscription databases not found on the "free" Net.

The following Web sites provide Internet evaluation criteria and learning activities. To help immigrants and English language learners, use Google's language tools to access that search engine in other languages. While the resultant sites may still be American, a simultaneous translation is usually provided.

Critical Evaluation Information
http://school.discovery.com/schrockguide/eval.html
This site contains a series of grade-specific evaluation forms and instructional materials.

Evaluating Information Found on the Internet
http://www.library.jhu.edu/researchhelp/general/evaluating/index.html
Johns Hopkins University Library site; treats the major factors to consider when evaluating information.

Evaluation (Detectives)
http://www.madison.k12.wi.us/tnl/detectives/evaluation.htm
A middle school library site on Internet evaluation and use.

Evaluation of Information Sources
http://www.vuw.ac.nz/staff/alastair_smith/evaln/evaln.htm
Part of the World Wide Web Virtual Library, this metasite links to many evaluation sources.

Internet Detective
http://www.sosig.ac.uk/desire/internet-detective.html
Interactive tutorial on evaluating the quality of Internet resources (English, French, Dutch versions).

Teen Zone
http://www.mrcpl.lib.oh.us/Teenzine/Web_Evaluations_Help.htm
Mansfield/Richland County Public Library's metasite on choosing and using Web sites.

Using the Internet for School Reports
http://www.quick.org.uk/menu.htm
Boston (Massachusetts) Public Library's guide for evaluating and using Internet sources.

Using Information

As with locating information, using information requires a number of skills: comprehension, interpretation, organization, and synthesis. To a large extent, as librarians, you have not been as involved in this part of information literacy, leaving it to classroom teachers who are subject experts. This picture is changing, though, as librarians point out the "protocols" for comprehending and producing different types of information, whether newspaper or hypertext. Indeed, the interplay of reading and writing works well as a way to approach different formats.

For instance, as teens make sense of a video and its visual "language," they are in a better position to create a video of their own; furthermore, if teens *start* by creating a video, they experience what works and what does not, so they come to appreciate the subtleties of video as they "read" it. Thus, libraries should provide production space as well as reading space, and you should help users understand how layout and textual patterns impact the communication of information.

Comprehension can be difficult for teens with language and literacy barriers, as well as for teens whose experiences do not intersect with the information encountered. For instance, teens from the tundra might have difficulty understanding the rain forest; rural teens might not understand inner-city issues; today's teens might have difficulty relating to medieval entertainment. The selection of manageable material is a first step, but at some point, teens need to be able to decipher information on their own. A number of technology tools can help in this regard: close-captioned television and video, recorded books, translation programs, scanning and reading software.

Increasingly, librarians and other educators are helping young people understand the *context* of the information by relating it to their personal lives and then providing background information so teens can fill in the cultural or experiential gaps. Therefore, you should acquire materials—and relevant URLs—that reflect your community, so users can see themselves in the collection and also make those mental transfers to other cultures.

One example is the Cinderella motif as it is retold in different cultures. For teens, that approach can be used to look at music and the arts in different countries, to see how dating and family life compare throughout the world, and to understand political realities in different nations. By offering different perspectives, you are helping young adults interpret information accurately and personally.

Multiple sources of information on the same subject can deepen teens' knowledge, and help them examine their world from several perspectives, which is part of their psychological development. However, trying to compare and organize these different sources into a logical and meaningful entity can be daunting. Technology can help in this endeavor by providing structures.

If files are available for downloading, teens can annotate them, reflecting on the messages and methods that those messages are expressed. Databases can be used to compare several similar entities such as people, things, places, and events; as teens "fill in the blanks" about each item, they can easily spot missing information and track it down.

Spreadsheets can be used to calculate numerical data and make predictions; that application can also be used in table display to create timelines and other ordered records. Teens with low verbal skills can create or find still and moving images that express their ideas and then organize them using drawing and editing software.

Collaborative efforts also help technologically disadvantaged teens. Each person brings his or her own experiences, perspectives, and skills to the task at hand. The visual eye of an English language learner can compensate for another's verbal skills; one can be organized without being textually literate while another can research but not write well. Technology tasks such as Web-page design can be subdivided into content, layout, and coding, for instance. The process of negotiating tasks is, in itself, an information literacy skill. Teamwork is a vital skill in the workplace, so learning how to apportion tasks equitably gives at-risk teens an employment edge.

Sharing and Acting on Information

One of the big turnoffs for at-risk teens is busy work. Their lives are full of drama and survival issues, so mundane reports on obscure topics written just for the teacher seem rather pointless. If teens are going to carve out time for doing research, there needs to be a payoff, and it needs to be more than grades. For that reason, designing learning activities that make a difference and draw on their experiences engages teens more, and results in better products.

Identifying a target audience for the product gives teens a mental "horizon point" to aim for. For instance, if teens know that collecting data about the quality of neighborhood water and researching water purification processes can help force a change in the procedures of public utilities, they may be more likely to dig deeper into the subject. Likewise, checking on current selective service draft laws, lowering the drinking age, finding out if it is necessary to contact parents when a girl is pregnant, are issues that have meaning for teens. Building on such research, if teens can broadcast their findings on the Internet or cable television, their voices—and their work—may be stronger. Again, the context of technology and its purpose makes a difference in its use and acceptance.

You can provide informational and communications resources for these projects most successfully when you work in concert with other entities such as the school community or local agencies. If your library hosts a Web site, teen work can be uploaded there. Your library can also sponsor a town hall gathering so teens can take their message to the people, and that event can be videotaped for local stations.

MEDIA LITERACY

Because teens are inundated with mass media messages every day, it makes sense for you, as a librarian, to help teens critically evaluate these messages and take appropriate action.

Media literacy may be considered a subset of information literacy, *except* that messages are taken in by the viewer often without their consent. Thus, rather than looking for information to address a problem or task, teens receive these messages almost unconsciously. Yet, they may react to those messages by buying a product or voting a particular way based on persuasive messages. This influence points out the other main concept about media messages: intent for profit or for power.

The Center for Media Literacy (http://www.medialit.org) posits five main processes when analyzing a media message:

1. Identify the producer.
2. Determine the attraction of the message.
3. Identify the points of view: what is included and what is omitted.
4. Determine the intent.
5. Create your own message or counteract the given message.

By being aware of mass media's intent, analyzing and reflecting on it, and then acting on it, teens gain more power over their environment. Media Literacy, Gender Equity (http://www.genderequity.org/medialit/

contents.html) has developed a curriculum guide that focuses specifically on gender issues as they relate to mass media.

Media literacy is particularly important to teens on the fringe of technology because it is direct evidence that technology has an impact on their lives—and that they *can* deal with technology on their own ground. Considering the number of mass media messages that vilify at-risk teens or their associated groups, it behooves teens to take back their own lives and leverage technology for their own purposes rather than someone else's.

You can approach teens and media literacy in several ways: bookmarking Web sites on media literacy, offering media literacy workshops, working with other agencies to educate teens about mass media messages, and helping teens create their own mass media messages.

INFORMATION LITERACY WEB SITES

The following Web sites provide good starting points in instructing teens about information literacy that incorporates technology.

CyberTours
http://www.infosearcher.com/cybertours
Librarian-developed interactive site for instruction and incorporation of the Web.

Directory of Online Resources for Information Literacy
http://bulldogs.tlu.edu/mdibble/doril
University of Florida's links to Webliographies, research, processes, organizations, programs, and tutorials.

Educator's Reference Desk: Information Literacy
http://www.eduref.org/cgi-bin/print.cgi/Resources/Subjects/Information_Literacy/Information_Literacy.html
A source for lesson plans, resources, Internet sources, and organizations.

ICT Literacy
http://www.ictliteracy.info
International initiative on information and communication technology literacy.

Information Literacy for K-16 Settings
http://www.csulb.edu/~lfarmer/infolitwebstyle.htm
This author's Web site offers step-by-step guidance in Big6 model research processes by integrating technology.

Information Skills Modules
http://www.lib.vt.edu/help/instruct/seven/library_research.html
Provides step-by-step instruction on doing research, specifically using online sources.

Library Research Guides
http://www.lib.berkeley.edu/TeachingLib/Guides
This site offers links to a series of library research guides developed by the library at the University of California, Berkeley, designed to show students how to use a variety of print and electronic resources.

OASIS: Online Advancement of Student Information Skills
http://oasis.sfsu.edu/
San Francisco (California) State University's series of interactive tutorials on information issues.

Skovde University Library (Sweden): Information Literacy
http://www.his.se/bib/enginfolit.shtml
Extensive international Web page listing contributions in the field of information literacy literature.

Washington Library Media Association: Information Literacy
http://www.wlma.org/Instruction/infolit.htm
This site links to several information literacy models, standards for several states, and curricula.

As teens become critical evaluators of technology, they can command more control of their environment. They can be more savvy consumers, and also help shape digital information. Libraries serve as the ultimate anticonsumerism watchdog and advocate for relevant and community-based information.

WORKS CITED

Farmer, L. (2001, January). Building information literacy through a whole school reform approach. *Knowledge Quest, 29*, 20–24.

8

DIGITAL CONTENT FOR TEENS

Keep it real
I have plenty of questions . . .
Health, sex, crime
Drugs, careers
The list is long . . .
Pregnancy, abortion
Gangs, on and on
Keep it real . . .
I need a say
Or I won't stay
My skills are weak
My reading too . . .
The task is large
So much at stake
Keep it real . . .

Jane Guttman

It's not simply a matter of getting people's hands on technology—in a sense, that's the easy part. Context is critical. The environment, the expectations, and what people bring to technology play major roles in what access really means on the ground.

Technology Counts 2001, 2001

RELEVANT CONTENT

In the final analysis, the main question relative to technology acceptance and use is: What's in it for me? At-risk teens are most apt to ignore technology if it does not meet their daily vital needs. Otherwise, trying to find the hardware and software, and learning how to use it seems pointless. What are those vital needs? Personal, educational, health-related, economic, entertaining, cultural, for starters.

Libraries can ensure that teens find the content that they need and want, whether through bookmarking or, preferably, providing links to relevant Web sites. Particularly for those teens who are not apt to darken the doors of libraries, providing Internet library portals with relevant links can entice tech fringers to browse the site and "bump" into a page on teen services and programs.

Although information "packaging" is a fairly new function, it fits in well with the technology environment. In this process, you should involve teens in identifying the types of content they want as well as specific Web sites that they like. Advisory groups are natural venues for this kind of input, but you should also reach out to elicit ideas from all teens through surveys, informal interactions, graffiti suggestion boards, and e-mail.

One unobtrusive way to get an idea of relevant Web sites with teen appeal is to check the history of Web site hits. For public libraries this can be accomplished in the late afternoon after teens have frequented the online computer stations.

In the meantime, the following Web sites focus on teen issues and have proven popular with teen users.

America's Teen.gov
http://www.afterschool.gov/kidsnteens2.html
Federal government site on teen issues, education, and the Internet.

Ask Dr. Jami
http://www.askdrjami.org
Addresses teens' concerns about resiliency.

BlackPlanet
http://www.blackplanet.com
The largest Internet destination for African Americans.

Chat the Planet
http://www.chattheplanet.com
Promotes global and cultural tolerance among teens through texts, multimedia content, and interaction.

Chicago Latino Network
http://clnet.sscnet.ucla.edu/
Directory of resources and services for Latinos.

Christian Teens
http://www.christianteens.net
Online resources and chat options for Christian teens.

End Nicotine Dependence
http://www.tobaccofreeutah.org/end.html
Resources for teens who want to stop smoking.

E-Subjects: Student Resources
http://www.esubjects.com/students/resources.html
Academic subject help.

Free Vibe
http://www.freevibe.com/drug_facts/alcohol.asp
Helps teens cope with family alcoholism.

Girls' Best Friend
http://www.girlsbestfriend.org/artman/publish/links_girls.shtml
Metasite of links for teen girls, with a focus on urban needs.

Health Links
http://healthlinks.healthology.com/teenhealth
Health issues for teens.

JavaNoir
http://www.javanoir.net/guide/index.html
African American resources on the Internet.

Juvenile Justice
http://www.pixelpress.org/juvenilejustice
Personal images and history about juvenile justice.

KidSpeak
http://www.kidspeakonline.org
Information for teens about First Amendment rights.

Money Matters
http://www.dcu.org/newmoney/money-matters-index.html
Consumer education program for teens.

Selected Youth Web Sites
http://www.scils.rutgers.edu/~kvander/websites.html
A directory for librarians of sites that would interest teens.

Stand Up Girl
http://standupgirl.com/
Support site on teenage pregnancy.

Teens 4 Hire
http://www.teens4hire.org
Search engine for teens to find jobs online.

YuHip
http://www.yuhip.org
Teen-savvy health issues, clinics, and job opportunities.

Local Information

For many "tech-not" teens, the world may well be confined to their neighborhoods. Thus, they may need local information that affects their day-to-day lives. Unfortunately, software tends to have a locale-neutral perspective. Percentage-wise, few Web sites focus on local needs; those that do are usually created and hosted by small community groups that might elude search engines.

You can transform your Roledex files of local information into an online database that is accessible from your library Web portal. Take advantage of teens' local knowledge by working with them in schools, housing projects, or recreation centers as an outreach function.

Have teens check the currency of information, get their input about local information, ask them to do data entry and help other teens translate information into their primary language. These are all ways to engage teens in meaningful information- and technology-rich experiences in library collaborations.

Two good directories of school library Web pages are: http://www.sldirectory.com/index.html#top and http://www.school-libraries.net. The following sample of public library Web portals targets local teens.

It's a Teen Thing!
http://www.peoriaaz.com/library/library_teen_sites.htm
Peoria (Arizona) Public Library Web site for teens.

Outernet
http://www.multicolib.org/outer
Multnomah County (Oregon) Library teen Web site available in English and Spanish; of special note is their list of local and national help for teens.

Real Life
http://www.clpgh.org/teens/index.html

Carnegie Library of Pittsburgh (Pennsylvania) site, created for teens, which includes homework help, reader's advisory, and work and volunteer opportunities.

Teen Page
http://www.ccpls.org/html/teens.html
Teen-developed site for Campbell County (Wyoming) Public Library.

TeenScape
http://www.lapl.org/teenscape/
Young Adults @ Los Angeles Public Library.

TeenSpace
http://teenspace.cincinnatilibrary.org
This site includes reading, homework help, and live library programs.

Teen Web Sites
http://www.wheaton.lib.il.us/library/teens/yawebsites.html
Wheaton (Illinois) Public Library sites for teens, including local interests.

Teen Zone
http://www.kcls.org/teens/
King County (Washington) Public Library Web portal addressing educational, cultural, and personal interests.

TeenZone
http://www.lib.ci.tucson.az.us/teenzone
Tucson-Pima (Arizona) Public Library Web portal; includes resources about course, local teen resource centers, advocacy, teen products, and online research help.

Education

Education is a major stumbling block for some teens, many of whom seldom use technology. Ironically, technology-enhanced courses can be a real lifesaver for these adolescents for several reasons:

- flexibility of time: teens can study whenever they have a free moment rather than 8 AM to 3 PM
- flexibility of pacing: teens control their own time to learn and submit assignments
- language: English language learners can consult dictionaries and use other means to understand and respond intelligently about the content

- content: sometimes local schools do not provide the courses that teens need and want, but an online course can offer an alternative way to learn
- social network: some teens may not relate well to their traditional peers, or may feel "stuck" or restricted in their present educational environment; an online environment lowers stereotyped barriers

School districts, particularly those that provide alternative educational options, and libraries can and should work together to provide online opportunities for teens on the social, educational, and technology fringe. Listed below are some Web sites that encourage nontraditional educational experiences.

Connecting Math to Our Lives International Project
http://www.orillas.org/math/index.html
Interactive site where young people gather data about math in their lives and report their findings.

Elsabio.com
http://www.elsabio.com
Spanish-language education portal.

Four Directions: An Indigenous Model
http://www.4Directions.org
This site uses technology to link culturally relevant concepts and educational environments to address the needs of at-risk Native American teens.

GED Information
http://www.acenet.edu/calec/ged/home.html
The official site for GED tests, it offers guidance for preparing and taking the exam.

Global Online Adventure Learning Site
http://www.goals.com
Educational adventures with an emphasis on science, technology, and nature.

Hotmath
http://www.hotmath.org
Free tutorial solutions for homework problems of popular textbooks.

If I Can Read, I Can Do Anything
http://www.ischool.utexas.edu/~ifican/index.html
Helps Indian communities increase literacy while preserving Native American identity; teens chat online to discuss books they have read with other Native American students, educators, and mentors.

National Center on Secondary Education and Transition
http://www.ncset.org
Helps parents of teens with disabilities to prepare them for high school and work.

New York Times Learning Network
http://nytimes.com/learning/index.html
Lessons are offered based on current events.

Teen Reading
http://www.ala.org/ala/yalsa/teenreading/teenreading.htm
Combination of information on teen reading and Teen Read Week.

UNESCO e-learning Portal
http://www.unesco.org/education/portal/e_learning/index.shtml
Includes free online courses and resources for elementary, secondary, and higher education.

Language Issues

Readability is another major issue for technology users. Content in English needs to be easy to read to address the needs of English language learners, yet mature enough to match their developmental stage. Currently, about 68 percent of Web content is in English; non-English Web sites and programs should be accessible for teens who read in other world languages, particularly since self-identification is linked to language usage (Warschauer, 2003).

However, language by itself is not sufficient; the content within that language still needs to address the interests and needs of teens. As suggested earlier, you can and should point out search engines with non-English options, such as Google. With this approach, teens can have more control in accessing the information they want. Again, for teens who tend not to enter the library building, having those Web sites on top in library portals eases access to information and also demonstrates that your library is sensitive to their needs. The following Web sites have information geared to English language learners and non-English speakers:

Activities for ESL Students
http://a4esl.org/
This site has ESL games.

Catherine Rifkin's Creative ESL Puzzles
http://www.geocities.com/Athens/Parthenon/5555/puzzle.html
This site has ESL games.

Comenius English Language Links
http://www.comenius.com/misc/links.php
This is a site for students and teachers of English.

Concentration Games for ESL Students
http://www.manythings.org/cg/
This site has ESL games.

Dave's ESL Café
http://www.eslcafe.com/
Internet meeting place for ESL/EFL students and teachers from around the world.

Digital Abiquiu
http://www.digitalabiquiu.com
This site is a community portal for northern New Mexicans.

Foreign Language Resources and Links
http://www.lll.uiuc.edu/resources/index.html
Search engines, reference sources, technology help, and foreign Web sites are found here.

Immigration and Naturalization Services Online
http://www.ins.usdoj.gov/
This site provides forms and fees information, forms by mail, answers to frequently asked questions, and contains a glossary and acronyms, among other services.

Infos Sur les Moteurs de Recherche
http://www.translatin.com/French/Liens.htm
These are search engines in French.

Internet Hotlist on Spanish Resources
http://www.kn.pacbell.com/wired/fil/pages/listspanish.html
Resources are grouped by broad educational level.

Mezzofanti
http://www.mezzofanti.org/translation/index.htm
This site lists free online translation search engines and dictionaries.

The National Network for Immigrant and Refugee Rights
http://www.nnirr.org/
Information is provided about local affiliates around the country and instructions for immigration assistance.

OPPulent pages for Students and Teachers of English as a Second Language
http://darkwing.uoregon.edu/~leslieob
Links to contemporary and cultural issues targeted to ESL populations.

Tareas Escolares
http://www.multcolib.org/libros/ref/sphomework.html
The Multnomah County (Oregon) Public Library Spanish-language homework site.

University of Illinois at Urbana-Champaign ESL Resources on the Web
http://www.iei.uiuc.edu/web.pages/esl.html
Grammar, listening and speaking, reading and writing, vocabulary, and collections of resources are found at this site.

CREATING CONTENT

As librarians, you can encourage all teens to be content providers, not just solely content consumers. In school settings, this approach is relatively easy to accomplish. Students can develop Web-based reports on current social issues, for instance. In the library they can write book and Web site reviews. Using schools, libraries, or youth-serving agencies as a catalyst—or by connecting independently—teens can collaborate with local community and business partners to develop a local Web presence, or produce broadcast-quality videos.

The easiest approach to incorporating teen content into library Web pages is, of course, to have teens submit their content in a form that is ready to evaluate and upload into a library's existing site. Ideally, you could use a teen panel to assess the value of the content and its appearance; in that way, teens who have little technology skills can still participate as content experts. You might need to work through other youth-serving agencies to get connected with those teens.

If you want to facilitate technical skills and know that your target teens can work in some public space, such as recreation centers or churches, consider a team approach: content expert, Web searcher, layout designer, and coder. Teens can build on their strengths and also train their peers in each aspect of developing Web content. An adult, whether librarian or other community technical specialist, should serve as an advisor to set expectations and parameters (some of which may be outside your control), make sure teens work well together, and monitor the project's progress.

If problems arise, the library's Web portal will not be jeopardized in the process. On the positive side, if teens have their own page, they will have more ownership of it, and may have greater control over its content and look; in any case, they will be more apt to publicize it and get other teens to use it.

Braun (2003) offers other specific tips for librarians working with teens to build Web pages. Dmoz, the Open Directory Project, provides a good list of sites on Web page design (http://dmoz.org/Kids_and_Teens/Computers/Web_Page_Design), and even notes free Web hosting services for teens who want to develop personal pages separate from the library. On the other hand, these same teens may also become motivated to use the library itself for the other resources and services that are available.

Jones and Pfeil (2004) lists twenty exemplary public library Web sites for teens. Listed below are a few other commendable Web sites that teens have created for their peers.

Adolescent Directory Online: Teens Only!
http://education.indiana.edu/cas/adol/teen.html
This site has links to teen writing as well as issues and leisure activities for teens.

Blue Jean Online
http://www.bluejeanonline.com
Written and produced by teen girls, this site includes personal experiences, creative writing, and resources for teens.

Girls Site Network
http://www.girlsite.org/
A forum for girls to network and share their stories.

Harlem Live
http://www.harlemlive.org
For and by teens, it addresses issues of race, community involvement, gender, and activism.

RepeatAfterUs
http://repeatAfterUs.com
Oral readings of English-language documents to use as an interactive English tutoring program; site developed by a 16-year-old-girl.

Spank
http://www.spankmag.com/
Youth culture defined by youth.

Teen Poetry
http://www.angelfire.com/co3/teenpoetry/home.html
Venue for teen writing and poetry contests.

Teens Online
http://personalweb.about.com/library/weekly/aa061801a.htm
Links to personal pages of teens.

ThinkQuest
http://www.thinkquest.org
An international competition where student teams engage in collaborative, project-based learning to create educational Web sites.

Tropical America
http://www.tropicalamerica.com
A free online game that explores 500 years of Latin American history; conceptualized by Los Angeles high school students and artists.

High-quality Web sites that focus on teen interests and issues can provide a teen-friendly way to become more comfortable about using technology to acquire information, to communicate, and to create and broadcast technology-based products. Links to projects that support technologically disadvantaged teens' involvement in career exploration and community-based action broaden their perspectives and give them places to make a difference.

Not only should you include such sites on your library Web site, but you should also "push" technology and associated learning activities by e-mailing the URLs of these sites to appropriate youth-serving agencies in a timely fashion. Similarly, these other agencies—along with original Web pages created by individual teens—may have valuable online content that can be publicized on the library's portal, which can also serve to advertise the contributions of nontraditional youth.

WORKS CITED

Braun, L. (2003). *Technically involved: Technology-based youth participation activities for your library*. Chicago: American Library Association.

Jones, P., & Pfeil, A. (2004, Spring). Public library YA Web pages for the twenty-first century. *YALS*, 14–18.

Technology Counts 2001. (2001, May 10). *Education Week*.

Warschauer, M. (2003). *Technology and social inclusion: Rethinking the digital divide*. Cambridge, MA: MIT Press.

9

USE OF TECHNOLOGY BY TEENS

Keep it simple
No Java for me
Think big
Help me with those
Speed bumps
Watch the "divide" disappear
When I get on that Internet
Give me IM any day
Okay, okay, so I'm not high-verbal
Keep me in mind for service learnin'
Hey, library lady
Open your doors
Show me those free services online
I can find online tutoring
And that 24/7 thing
Think big
Keep it simple
No child left behind
That means me . . .

Jane Guttman

By now it should be apparent that sustained technology use requires a set of resources and skills. Technologically disadvantaged teens need access, technical skills, and intellectual tools to assess and use technology-enhanced resources, as well as meaningful content. Yet even with all these necessary elements, some teens become technology dropouts. Interestingly, the major sticking point is usually social. Let us examine the factors that facilitate *and* impede technology use so you can help teens become successful technology users.

DEVELOPMENT OF TECHNOLOGY USE

Sustained technology use requires a series of successful interactions and persistence when faced with technology obstacles. At any point along the way, teens may choose to opt out of the process. In the final analysis, they need to be shown that obstacles can be overcome because support is available, and that the eventual payoff is worth the time and effort.

In the best-case cycle, technology users begin by looking for applications and resources that meet their own self-interests. Perhaps they need legal or health information or they need to create a resume or perhaps they want to pursue a hobby. Their use of technology resembles a consumer mentality. Over time, technology use involves interaction with others, if for no other reason than to get technical assistance. Usually, though, technological interaction arises when teens request information from a Web site or when someone wants to e-mail them a file.

The next step often involves *creating* information or documents; teens at this point are actually contributing to the world of technology. With sustained technology success, teens start to change their self-perceptions and their relationships. Their human network gets larger as they make connections to new groups. More opportunities become available as a result, so teens experience personal freedom and a greater sense of control. In the process, teens have an opportunity to remake themselves in order to fulfill their desires and then they can identify new wishes (Katz, Rice, & Aspden, 2001).

Some teens start to use technology, particularly the Internet, but then stop. Basically, if any point during the process becomes a bottleneck, teens who are not persistent may well walk away. Money is a major barrier to buying equipment and software as well as paying for ongoing services. Even with a free Internet account, if teens have no one to e-mail (i.e., no friends or family), then they will not use that service. If public access is unpredictable or a constant hassle, they will get turned off. Furthermore, if the hardware and software seem too complex to learn, some teens will become frustrated and quit (Lenhart, 2003).

Internet use, in itself, does not have an impact on motivation or barriers. Instead, Internet dropouts—and technology dropouts in general—tend to have less expertise, and are younger, poorer, and less educated (Compaine, 2001).

You can help teens overcome these technological "speed bumps" by being available to provide coaching and identify other sources of help. Of course, it makes sense to start with technology applications that require minimal training and support so teens can feel successful quickly. Proactively, you can provide links to online tutorials on your Web portal and identify technical experts. Give contact information so teens can get the help they need when they need it.

Of course, as a resource center, your library can make every effort to provide enough hardware, at a satisfactory level of operation, to satisfy local teens' needs. Software and Internet connectivity are also needed to enable teens to have successful technology experiences.

INDEPENDENT TECHNOLOGY USE

Just because teens have access to computers and telecommunications does not mean that they will focus their activities on educational or other self-improvement pursuits. Sometimes, in poor and minority households teens are more likely to use technology for games and other entertainment than to support academics (Wilhelm, Carmen, & Reynolds, 2002). Part of that difference in usage may stem from lack of knowledge about useful resources and applications; it may stem from misconceptions about technology that it is a "White Man's job"; it may stem from lack of technical skills; or it may stem from family or community values. Still, use of the Internet and computers at work is a good indicator of computer and Internet use at home (U.S. Department of Commerce, 2002). Optimally, teens would have home technology access to relevant content, reinforced through family involvement, with technology support.

As noted in the Introduction, teens use of technology ranges from schoolwork to entertainment, from e-mail to online chat. As teens get older, they tend to play fewer games and conduct more adultlike searches, reflecting their psychological development. However, within this larger picture, specific differences in technology use start to emerge when considering subpopulations.

Figure 9.1
Major Activities among Children and Young Adults, 2001 as a Percentage of U.S. Population under 25 Years Old

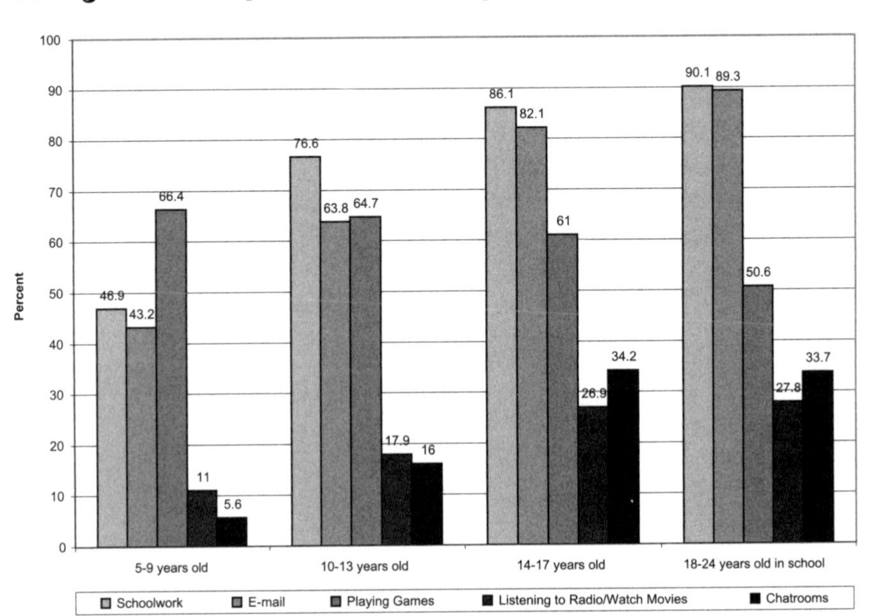

Source: NTIA and ESA, U.S. Department of Commerce, using U.S. Census Bureau Current Population Survey Supplements (U.S. Department of Commerce, 2002, p. 53).

The most obvious one is gender. While girls now comprise the majority of Internet users, they use the medium differently from boys. Girls use the Internet more for education and communication, while boys use it more for entertainment (National School Boards Foundation, 2003). Generally, girls see computers as a means, not an end, as do boys. Similarly, girls see technology as an activity that involves other people while boys focus on controlling the machinery. Girls' attitudes about technology become critical in the adolescent years, although their opinions are formed earlier on.

Hackbarth (2001) found that fourth grade girls had the same positive attitudes toward computers as boys, but were less likely to have access to computers outside the school and were less likely to use computers to do projects; therefore, their technical vocabulary and ability lagged. Additionally, the social pressures on pubescent girls start to affect technology access and use. Boys spend more time on computers, and parents tend to buy boys their own computers more than they purchase them for girls.

The 2000 report of the American Association of University Women on girls and technology found that girls were not technophobic; rather, they did not like the computer *culture*. They found programming the computer to be boring, they did not like the nature of most computer games, and they saw few positive adult female role models. Instead, the report found that girls prefer telecommunications and open-ended, creative software.

Ironically, as females use telecommunications more, some males are starting to shun the Internet as a "girlie" thing (Lenhart, 2003). Other subgroups exhibit certain patterns. Social groups such as gangs, who perceive themselves as outside the establishment, may reject technology use as a concrete symbol of Otherness—although some gangs recruit via the Internet. Poor teens may think that the Internet is frivolous and impractical. Some ethnic or religious groups may reject the values portrayed in many sites. English language learners may be intimidated by the number of English-only sites. Illiterates realize very quickly the degree to which the Internet is textual and may feel frustrated or ashamed that they cannot take advantage of the information found there. Teens with disabilities often do not want to "stand out" so may choose not to use high-profile assistive technology. There are probably as many reasons that teens may *not* use technology as *would* use technology. Somehow, the benefits have to outweigh the negatives.

TEEN TECHNOLOGY USE IN SCHOOLS

The 2002 reauthorization of the Elementary and Secondary Education Act of 1965 was renamed the No Child Left Behind Act (NCLB) and is proving to have a sweeping impact on education. The Educational Technology program, Enhancing Education Through Technology (E2T2), was folded into the NCLB, indicating the federal government's seriousness about technology and its incorporation into the curriculum. Technology was viewed as an important aid in helping students meet academic standards, facilitating distance education, promoting parent involvement, and supporting evaluation. States are required to submit technology plans to demonstrate how they will use their technology money, and 50 percent of those funds must be allocated to Title I (high poverty) schools to address issues of equity access.

The technology standards established by the International Society for Technology in Education (ISTE), provide a useful framework for examining teen use of technology in schools. However, their implementation depends on each academic setting. Schools, by their very nature, impact student use of technology, just as they impact reading habits. Historically, technology has been approached as a separate domain, in which students learned how to operate equipment and program computers. On the other end of the spectrum, students used drill-and-kill software. While basic operations ability is still needed, the current emphasis on academic technology use is purposeful. Thus, teens can access information beyond the textbook, capture and manipulate that information, and then communicate their learning using technology.

A number of practices offer especially powerful ways to engage teens who are underserved technologically. Students more successfully navigate the Internet when they are not asked to account for their strategies, but rather can explore independently. Likewise, what students consider a success may differ from that of adults, and the latter need to be more flexible about their expectations. If students *feel* successful, they are more likely to use technology in the future, and further, they have a greater likelihood of improving their skills.

Building on the importance of community, educators can provide and design opportunities for teens to coach each other and younger students. For example, teens can interview relatives and community members using audio- or videotapes to produce oral histories. However, since teen use largely depends on physical access to appropriate technology, and teens on the fringe of technology often live in technology-poor communities and attend low-tech schools (or do not attend school at all), these efforts may not reach them.

Of particular importance in schools is reading and writing. Within that framework, computer-mediated communication (CMC) can play a significant role in helping teens become literate. CMC software typically exists in two forms: synchronous chat mode, where students can share their written expressions and receive immediate feedback, and asynchronous exchanges, where messages are posted for later response. In both cases, emphasis is placed on the social activity of reading and writing. This approach particularly helps English language learners, the physically disabled, and others who are not high-verbal learners, because it enables students to think about their content and the way to express it without the constraints of time or face-to-face discomfort and vulnerability. CMC also facilitates collaborative projects because students can share and comment on documents more easily, and archive their activities. On the other hand, increased anonymity can foster off-track and offensive comments; so adult monitoring is needed to curb inappropriate behavior and clarify expectations (Reinking et al., 1998).

The gap between social and academic use of technology also echoes general literacy practices and values. When the dominant culture devalues informal, out-of-school activities, it is harder to bridge the two worlds.

Service Learning

Service learning is one way to link the social and academic use of technology. This practice encourages teens to "test" abstract concepts introduced in school by conducting a reality check in the local community, preferably by volunteering to help a local agency by applying what was learned academically. In terms of technology, for instance, students who learn Web design could develop sites to publicize nonprofit organizations. Similarly, videotaping skills can be used in the community to shadow businesses as a career exploration activity. If teens see inequities in their community, they can use technology to research viable solutions and present strong cases to local authorities. Thus, service learning can increase a sense of citizenship and provide public recognition for positive skills and actions.

Best Practice

The following projects reflect the best practice of teen use of technology in support of academics.

Cyber-reading
http://www.DearReader.com
Subscribers receive e-mail each day for a five-minute segment of a book; the service includes an online reader's advisory, online teen book review and a book club.

Generation YES
http://www.genyes.org
Trains teens in technology skills so they can work with teachers and community members to help infuse technology into the curriculum and maintain networks. A separate program, GEN GIT (Girls' Issues and Technology) targets girls who are reluctant tech users.

iEARN
http://www.iearn.org/projects
This lists projects in more than one hundred countries where young people work collaboratively across borders to improve their communities.

Student Tech Corps
http://www.studenttechcorps.org
A Dell Computers-sponsored program to train middle school students to run tech support help desks in schools.

Students' Take
http://www.thirteen.org/edonline/studentstake
Produced by students for the school community, this project provides a place for students to speak out on issues affecting their lives. Each month, students create an original Web piece, often including interviews, video, articles, graphics, interactive features, and more, based on a thought-provoking theme.

Telementors
http://www.clmer.csulb.edu/clmer/learn_net_comm.asp
Groups pre- and in-service teachers, parents and teens to develop community-based projects such as environmental justice.

TEEN TECHNOLOGY USE IN LIBRARIES

Libraries play a significant role in teens' use of technology, whether in a community or school setting. Either way, the library is considered a public area where teens can have some freedom in choosing how to use these tools. Still, some regulations do exist: the amount of time teens can be on the system, to some extent the nature of the content to be accessed, the amount of printing allowed, and the noise level permitted. In school settings, e-mail and chat may also be curtailed, for technical and legal reasons.

The public nature of libraries also fosters social interaction with peers and other generations. Teens may want to share content that they find or create; they might help others troubleshoot problems; they might develop a document together. In the process, they may have to take turns using technology and negotiate priority use, which may be more difficult in public libraries where that process is more likely to be done between strangers. In school libraries, that prioritization is usually predicated on assignment deadlines; in public libraries, access is typically controlled by a time-delineated, sign-up procedure.

In Loertscher and Woolls' (2002) study on teen use of libraries, one of the top three activities was Internet use. The Gates Library Program

Figure 9.2
Computer Use in Libraries by Percent of Teens

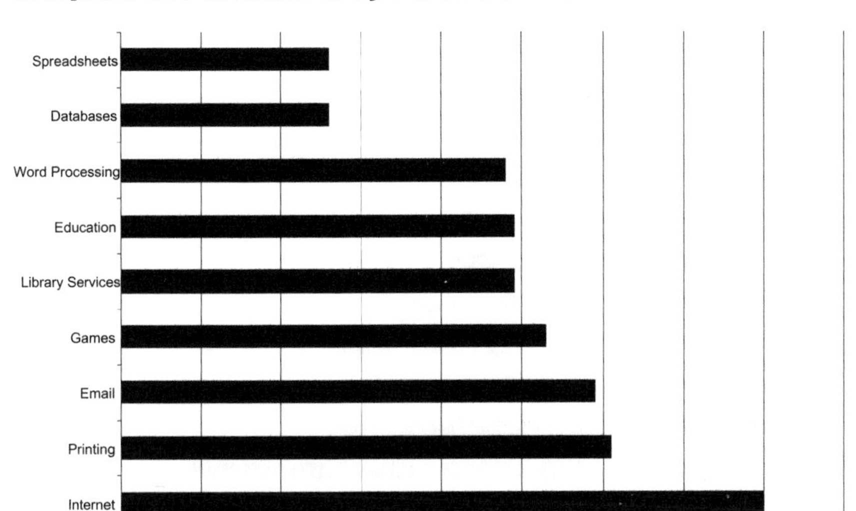

(http://www.gatesfoundation.org/Libraries) provided public access computers in public libraries within five states. In a report to the foundation on the public's use of these systems (Moore et al., 2002), it was found that teens were the greatest users. Teens also visited the library more often and stayed longer than adults. Minorities made up 46 percent of teen users, as opposed to 20 percent of adult users.

According to the Loertscher and Woolls study, teens also used computers as a social activity, visiting with each other at adjacent computer stations, exhibiting behavior that differed from that of adults. Most teens felt comfortable using the computers, and almost all asked the librarian when they needed help. In turn, teens sometimes helped adult patrons and librarians.

A variety of public and school libraries offer a number of other library technology services that teens use, including:

- 24/7 reference service
- e-books
- videotaping of community landmarks
- videotaping and audiotaping of oral histories
- online tutoring

Figure 9.3
Web Site Use by Percent of Teens

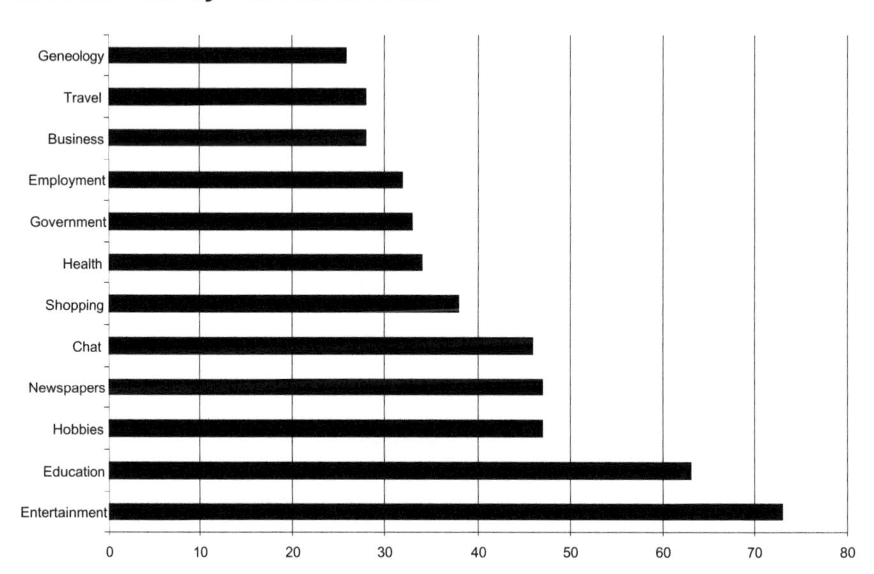

- online book discussion groups
- virtual library space
- technology training
- Web design

In the previously cited Loertscher and Woolls study, it was found that another major reason that teens used the library was to volunteer their time and services. Schools and public librarians increasingly engage teens in community projects that involve technology. They gain technical expertise as well as contribute to the civic well-being of the community. Teens can act as technology coaches and tutors, install software and troubleshoot technical problems, help create and maintain library or community databases and Web pages, and produce print and nonprint documents.

In these volunteer capacities, teens should be treated in the same way as they would be for nontechnology, or paid positions; they should be interviewed, trained, supervised, and supported. In high-security jobs, such as system troubleshooting or network uploading, you must carefully consider before giving teens such access, not only because teens might be pressured by their peers to do something inappropriate, but also because if a snafu occurs, both the teen and the adult will be held responsible. In either case, you both may be in a possibly overwhelming situation.

Libraries for the Future has developed a clearinghouse of programs developed by libraries in partnership with community and business groups. Programs of particular relevance are Youth Access, Health Access, Education Access, and Reading America (http://www.lff.org/programs). Queens (New York), Brooklyn (New York), and Chicago (Illinois) public libraries are particularly well known for their strong teen programs that incorporate technology. In addition, the following projects exemplify powerful teen use of technology in library settings:

- An after-school technology program in the Austin (Texas) Public Library provides at-risk teens with equipment and kid-friendly software on a first-come, first-served basis. Librarians and educators help teens learn and showcase their technology skills. Teens use computers for e-mail, e-pals, homework, tutoring, and leisure activities.
- Flint (Michigan) Public Library coordinates a year-long, intensive after-school technology program where at-risk students learn to use a variety of technology tools and then work with community members to develop Web sites. (Durrance & Fisher, 2003)
- Valencia (Arizona) Public Library coordinates an e-journalism program for teens who are largely Latino. Teens learn about the publishing business and produce teen-zines and newsletters (http://aleyda2.tripod.com). Neighboring Santa Rosa Learning Center Library, located next to public housing projects, also started a teen-zine program.

TEEN TECHNOLOGY USE IN COMMUNITIES

Teens also connect independently with community centers and agencies to use technology. In fact, public use of technology has become a new vehicle for social community building. Leveraging teens' recreational and personal interests, the venues for such use are growing in:

- parks and recreation centers
- youth-serving agencies (e.g., Boys and Girls Clubs, YMCA/YWCA)
- housing projects

- museums
- shopping mall kiosks
- Internet cafés
- video gaming centers

Residential and recreational centers increasingly provide computers and Internet connectivity. This practice facilitates technology training and lifelong learning across generational lines, ultimately uniting and empowering its constituents. One of the strengths of community-based technology use is its informal nature; grades and salaries are not at stake. This approach attracts teens, and provides a means for them to receive social networking support. In the process, they also gain responsibility and become a meaningful part of the community.

As community entities provide technology for use by young people, they should consider the following factors:

- Leadership: Who will provide vision, build support, and coordinate the program?
- Decision making: Who will make decisions, and what will be the process?
- Purpose: What will be the objective of the technology center and its use? What does the community need, and what does it value?
- Policies: What policies, rules, and regulations need to be established, and who will enforce them?
- Funding: What kind of budget is needed, what funding sources are available, and how will the money be managed?
- Programs and services: What services will be provided, on what basis, and for whom? What material resources are needed, and how will they be acquired and maintained?
- Personnel: What staffing is needed, on what basis, for what purpose?
- Training: What will be the content and extent of training, who will provide it, and who will receive training?
- Context: What political, economic, social, and educational contexts influence the project?
- Equity: How will equitable participation be insured?

In each case, communities must consider the roles that teens can and will play. How are teens' needs and interests identified? To what extent will teens' opinions be garnered and acted on? What decisions will teens be able to make? What leadership roles can they play? What will be the extent and nature of their influence on other community members?

A sampling of ways teens can contribute includes:

- gathering information about youth and other community constituents
- organizing community information
- publicizing efforts
- identifying and comparing hardware and software
- setting up systems and installing software
- developing training material and "piloting its delivery" in workshops for staff or community members
- coaching other community members

As a librarian, you can optimize teens' use of technology by referring them to appropriate community entities. Additionally, you and community members can cosponsor training sessions and create community-based Web portals. By using local human resources, you can strengthen your partnerships within the community and provide other library services to augment technology.

Need some ideas on ways to collaborate? The following community-based projects advance teens' use of technology and bolster youth participation in the community.

Boston Photo Collaborative
http://www.bostonphoto.org/programs.html

Programs teach teens about photography and help them develop business capabilities; the collaborative also supports after-school programs for unstructured exploration, with staff, volunteers, and digital artists available to help teens.

Ecologies of Children's Computing: Investigating the Use of Technology Across Multiple Settings
http://www2.edc.org/CCT/projects_summary.asp?numProjectId=829

In an effort to learn how they think about and use technology, the Center for Children and Technology uses teens as informants and research collaborators, exploring the role that technology plays in their communities and in their lives.

FLOC New Technology Center
http://www.flocdc.org/tech_cen.htm
A state-of-the-art media center where Washington, DC, teens learn communications technology, personal development, and entrepreneurial skills. Teens explore the world of art and ideas by creating videos, animation, Web pages, digital music, and computer graphics.

Jewish Community Center, St. Paul (Minnesota)
http://www.stpauljcc.org/teens.html
This low-income, community teen lounge provides computer time to do homework and explore technology. The center's technology program includes a mentoring program to teach computer skills, with teens paired with senior citizens, people with disabilities, and people who do not speak English as their first language (e.g., Russian, Laotian, and Spanish).

National Urban Technology Center: Youth Leadership Academy
http://www.urbantech.org/yla_home.cfm
A 180-hour training program that intertwines computer learning with development of social skills. A school-to-work component introduces teens to the world of work through computer simulations.

Playing2Win
http://www.playing2win.org
This community technology center in Harlem supports multimedia projects built by teens.

STRUGGLE project at Pittsburgh's Community House
http://www.pgh-inet.org/bb/community_house.html
Using an apprentice approach, poor minority teens and adults write online about their experiences and struggles using computers. Technology provides more objectivity as they communicate and negotiate consensus on implications and resolutions.

Union City: A Virtual Tour
http://www2.edc.org/CCT/projects_summary.asp?numProjectId=640
A sophisticated technical infrastructure provides a self-sustaining human network for creative and effective use of Web resources for teaching and learning.

Young Webmasters Program
http://www.techlearning.com/db_area/archives/WCE/archives/stay/lor.html
Young Webmasters programs combine training in Web design and academics for needy teens.

Zeum
http://www.zeum.org
A hands-on technology center for youth enables teens in a disadvantaged area of San Francisco (California) to create digital multimedia productions, such as online historical or science information.

In the final analysis, you can help teens take greater control of their lives by being in control of technology. The message that you want to send is that teens have a voice and that they can take advantage of technology to use that voice to express themselves, to improve themselves, and to improve the world they want to live in.

WORKS CITED

American Association of University Women. (2000). *Tech-savvy: Educating girls in the new computer age*. Washington, DC: AAUW.

Compaine, B. (Ed.). *The digital divide: Facing a crisis or creating a myth?* Cambridge, MA: MIT Press.

Durrance, J., & Fisher, K. (2003). Determining how libraries and librarians help. *Library Trends, 51*(4), 541–570.

Hackbarth, S. (2001, April). Changes in primary students' computer literacy as a function of classroom and gender. *Tech Trends, 45*(4), 19–27.

Katz, J., Rice, R., & Aspden, P. (2001, November). The Internet, 1995–2000: Access, civic involvement, and social interaction. *American Behavioral Scientist, 45*(3), 405–419.

Lenhart, A. (2003). *The ever-shifting Internet population: A new look at Internet access and the digital divide*. Washington, DC: The Pew Internet and American Life Project. http://www.pewinternet.org/pdfs/PIP_Shifting_Net_Pop_Report.pdf.

Loertscher, D., & Woolls, B. (2002, May). Teenage users of libraries. *Knowledge Quest, 30*(5), 31–36.

Moore, E., et al. (2002). *It's working: People from low-income families disproportionately use library computers*. Seattle, WA: University of Washington.

National School Boards Foundation. (2003). *Safe and smart*. Alexandria, VA: National School Boards Foundation.

Reinking, M., et al. (Eds.). *Handbook of literacy and technology*. Mahwah, NJ: Erlbaum.

U.S. Department of Commerce. (2002). *A nation online: How Americans are expanding their use of the Internet*. Washington, DC: U.S. Department of Commerce. http://www.ntia.doc.gov/ntiahome/dn/.

Wilhem, T., Carmen, D., & Reynolds, M. (2002). *Connecting kids to technology: Challenges and opportunities*. Baltimore, MD: Annie E. Casey Foundation. http://www.aypf.org/forumbriefs/2002/fb071802.htm.

10

A CALL TO ACTION

So I wanted to save the future
So I became a librarian—
So I wanted to touch teens' soles
So I dug what they really needed—
So I wanted to bridge the digital gap
So I wired a room—
So I wanted to empower the fringers
So I opened their minds—
So they wanted more skills
So they grabbed my attention—
So they wanted more time
So they took over the schedule—
So they wanted to create
So they pushed for more RAM—
So they wanted their say
So they broadcast their words
So the public complained
So the staff glared at us
So control crashed and burned
So norms cracked and fell
So who really wants change?

Lesley Farmer

The future of our teens is at stake, and technology can make the difference. More specifically, libraries can serve as a safe conduit between technology and teens who may be typically underserved. Are you ready?

PROCEDURES FOR ACTION

Let's review the process.

1. Know yourself and your library. Provide high-quality, professional service with the resources you have. Interact effectively and enthusiastically with teens. Assess the library's mission and potential and to plan strategically. Build library capacity and conditions for change so the system can adjust successfully.
2. Know your community. Who lives and works there? What demographics are reflected? How has the community changed over time, and why? Assess its assets, human and tangible, by examining documents, visiting sites, talking with a variety of people. Specifically, look at technology's presence (or absence) and role in the community.
3. Identify teens who are left out of, or underserved, by the technology revolution. What demographic patterns emerge? What subgroups can be identified? What is the basis for nonuse: lack of physical access, barriers to intellectual access, perceptions about technology? There may well be differences in technology use between subgroups, so careful data gathering and analysis of each population must be done. Ask teens, parents, schools, and community members about perceived exclusions or persistent needs.
4. Identify other youth-serving agencies. Specifically, contact those organizations in the community that serve "tech-not" teens, and that might collaborate or partner in technology endeavors. What resources do they bring to the table: technology, financial backing, staffing, networking skills, knowledge about teens and the community? What common goals can be met through collaboration? Help create policies and align efforts to facilitate change.
5. Identify "tech-not" teens' needs and interests. For example:
   - health information: nutrition and eating disorders, sexuality, birth control and pregnancy, HIV, infections, diseases, smoking, substance abuse, AA and other support groups; symptoms and treatments; local agencies

- finances: money management, financial aid, credit
- employment: job openings, applications, job fairs, information about careers, volunteer opportunities, interviewing skills, communication skills
- education: subject matter, writing skills, study skills, homework help, tutors and tutorials
- civil rights and political activism: immigrants' rights, citizenship processes, voting, driving rules, student rights, lobbying, advocacy, laws and regulations, legal advice, politics, campaigning
- computer and video gaming: systems, software, playing techniques, development skills, networking
- entertainment: sports, music, video, art, reading, writing, performance, production
- hobbies: collecting, trading, crafts, modelling, photography and other imaging, reenactments, specialized subjects

In each case, technology can facilitate accessing and sharing information through e-mail, chat, IM, blogging, videoconferencing, audiotapes, videotapes, multimedia presentations, Web tutorials, online experts, databases of organizations, simulations, and billions of informational documents.

6. Review your current library services and brainstorm ideas to extend services to meet the needs of "tech-not" teens. Clubs that incorporate technology might include:
   - tech aide club: learning and applying technology skills by coaching library users and assisting classroom teachers
   - video club: learning or teaching video production skills, viewing or creating videos, videotaping as a service to community groups
   - local cable television station community production crew: helping to produce teen, library, or community-based shows; broadcasting nonprofit videos of interest to teens
   - photography club (particularly if it involves digital photography): learning or teaching film or digital photography skills; viewing, creating, or editing film and digital photos; creating photo collections (including CDs or DVDs); displaying teen or other community photos
   - animation club: producing and showing original works using pixilation, claymation, Flash, and other software programs

- Web design club: learning or teaching video Web design skills; creating, modifying, or updating personal, library, or community Web sites
- Think Quest competition (http://www.thinkquest.org): producing educational interactive learning activities
- Technology Student Association (http://www.tsawww.org): a national organization that promotes technology for young people through high school
- technology mentoring programs (particularly for girls): learning or teaching technology skills; helping teens learn about technology careers; providing technology career advice; offering internships

Possible services might include:

- homework centers: to help teens and as a means for teens to help youngsters
- tutoring services: to help teens and as a means for teens to help youngsters
- venues for cultural expressions via technology: video productions, electronic music, digital publications and imaging, audiocassettes, photography exhibits, and so on
- online publishing: to help teens learn and teach skills, to provide venues for teens to self-publish and for the community
- interactive telecommunication: chats, IMing, Webcams, blogging
- technology job fairs: to help teens explore careers and get job leads
- technology shows: to show teens the newest technology; to provide a means for teens to buy/sell/trade electronics; to enable teens to demonstrate their knowledge about technology
- technology career advice: to help teens explore careers and determine appropriate preparation for technology-related careers

7. After careful consideration of resources available and teens' needs, decide on programs that are feasible for your library and community (with or without partners). Which services will be most effective in meeting teens' needs and supporting the library mission? What can be done with existing resources and staffing? Can resources be reallocated to provide those services? What efforts

would require additional resources, and how might those resources be found? What services might be possible if done in collaboration with another entity, such as a community center, business, educational institution, or nonprofit organization? Create an action plan and schedule for your program.

8. Prepare library administration and staff to handle new services and programs. What policies, procedures, and forms need to be reviewed, modified, or added? What priorities need to be changed, and how will that affect existing resources and services? Who will lead the effort, who will be responsible and accountable? What staff development is needed in terms of new skill sets, new procedures, or different dispositions when working with underserved teens? How will partnerships with other entities be handled? How will changes be communicated; do communication channels need to be modified or added?
9. Promote your programs and new services through established and alternative means, for example:
   - via foreign language media: local newsletters and newspapers, radio stations, public access television, community listservs
   - through community social agencies and programs: social services, GED and ESL programs, housing projects, homeless shelters, religious centers, detention centers
   - at sites where "tech-not" teens hang out: eateries, shopping areas, public centers, recreation areas, "service" stores (e.g., beauty shops, gas stations, repair shops)
   - by doing "tech-talks" at underserved schools or other organizations where "tech-not" teens gather.
10. Add services and/or programs, remaining flexible to, and accommodating, specific needs of participants. Find out the best days of the week and time for conducting programs, considering after-hour library service. Have translators for non-English speakers. Provide babysitting for teen parents. Offer single-sex tech workshops where appropriate. Make assistive technology and tech aides available for teens with physical challenges. Find ways to make the library gang-neutral. Provide transportation such as free bus passes. Bring the program or service to teens via a tech bus. These accommodations cost money, but may constitute an authentic basis for community-based collaborations and partnerships.

11. Assess, evaluate, and begin planning the next step. Both the process and the outcome should be examined along the way and at the end. Think in terms of the teens served, the library, partners, the community, and the technologies. From the beginning, identify what and who will be evaluated—and why, what are valid and reliable assessment instruments, and data gathering processes (when, where, how, who). If possible, get baseline data at the start so you can measure changes after implementing the new service or program. Once the data are analyzed, communicate the results to decision makers and stakeholders, including teens. Then act on the assessments in order to maximize the library's impact on teens. The goal is sustainable programs.

BEST PRACTICE

When creating your plan, look to other programs for inspiration and guidance. Build on their experiences to create the best possible program for your library and community. Following are examples of successful library programs and services that have helped meet the technological needs of underserved teens.

Enoch Pratt Public Library's Community Youth Corps (Baltimore, Maryland) trains teens to serve as technology assistants. They also develop public programs in collaboration with college mentors (http://www.smartlink.org/cyc_desc.cfm). Their site also includes links to teen-related sites for babysitting, health and fitness, sports, sexuality, homework help, and so forth. Enoch Pratt also provides "Night Owl" telephone reference services. Neighboring Baltimore County (Maryland) Public Library (BCPL) provides digital reference service through AskUsNow! (http://askusnow.info). This system tried to provide free Internet accounts but slow connections and outdated equipment made virtual reference difficult on-site.

San Francisco (California) Public Library provides online career and education planning. The main branch offers daily guidance on colleges, financial aid, and tutoring (http://sfpl.lib.ca.us/sfplonline/teen/teens.htm).

Youth Access Projects, sponsored by Libraries for the Future, trains library staff and supports after-school programming for teens in the areas of technology skills, access to electronic resources, literacy development, and creative expression (http://www.lff.org/programs/youth.html). Examples of programs include e-journalism, MyHero zine, interactive science and engineering skills, and GIS mapping.

Boston (Massachusetts) Public Library offers "Real Time": tutoring in mathematics, linking eighth graders with local college students who communicate via computer microphones (http://www.bpl.org/general/foundation).

Austin (Texas) Public Library established "Wired for Youth," an after-school drop-in program for at-risk, low-income youth to facilitate Internet and computer access. Their youth-only centers include workshops, tutoring, and homework help. WFY also showcases teen work, enrolls youth in e-pal programs, and provides support in Spanish. A private foundation underwrites these centers.

"Educate the Child" Foundation distributes more than $20 million in educational materials and technology. One of their recipients, Franklin Middle School Library (Long Beach, California), raises students' level of opportunities through this ongoing support (http://www.lbusd.k12.ca.us/franklin/index.htm).

Santa Ana (California) High School Library wanted to use technology to help inner-city students connect with their culture and community. As Library of Congress American Memory Fellows, the library media teacher and Spanish teacher developed a Mexican American Studies research project based on the community's food, buildings, and celebrations. Students researched how to locate background information on the Internet and electronic periodical database and used digital cameras to capture local culture. They also analyzed the *California's Gold* video series to learn interviewing skills and then gathered information from community members. They published their results at http://www.creativeinsites.net/sahsweb/msanchez/mexam.html.

ConnectNet/Conectado tells teens where public Internet access is available (http://www.ConnectNet.org). It is the result of sponsorship by Time Warner and the Digital Divide Network. Librarians were trained in its use, and public service announcements were developed to disseminate information about this service.

Tucson-Pima (Arizona) Public Library focuses on its 85 percent Latino teen population, enabling youth to videotape and write about their community. Their e-zine program is funded by a corporate grant, and is part of the Youth Access e-journalism program created by Libraries for the Future.

Queens Borough (Queens, New York) Public Library's New American program offers multilingual Web sites and streaming public programming on cultural arts and coping skills. The library is seen as a safe, welcoming location, and helps immigrants connect with the local community (http://www.queenslibrary.org). The system also received a juvenile justice grant to mentor at-risk teens and lead them to appropriate library programs such as science video conferences, community activism workshops, and body image advice. The Queens' district attorney's office meets with the library to suggest improvements.

Multnomah County (Oregon) Public Library maintains a teen online presence: Outernet (http://www.multcolib.org/outer/help.html). It includes national and local helplines as well as information on careers, college, homework, health, entertainment, and technology. The system also provides a Spanish-language homework site (http://www.multcolib.org/libros/ref/sphomework.html).

Los Angeles (California) County's Office of Education Distance and Online Education program provided laptops for the children of migrant farmworkers. The students could also access online resources at public libraries through their accounts. A cybrarian served as a stable information guide regardless of the students' locale (http://www.lacoe.edu/orgs/92/index.cfm). This service was eliminated when budgets were cut.

The Dragonfly Project, the result of a partnership between the Haines Public Library and the Chilkoot Indian Association (Haines Borough, Alaska), teaches library-related technology skills to 11- to 21-year-olds, who then serve as transgenerational tech mentors. A grant from the Institute of Museum and Library Services underwrote the original project. Teens are also learning video skills by producing short movies about Tlingit life. As a result of these efforts, tech mentors have portfolios, which reflect their abilities and self-confidence and will help them in future endeavors. Additionally, the project has increased library use and strengthened the sense of community (http://haineslibrary.org/haineslibrary/dragonfly/index.html).

Dallas (Texas) Public Library's Teen Wise Centers focus on providing positive activities for teens who are at risk for dropping out, joining gangs, or becoming teen parents. Computers, games, tutoring, speakers, and forums attracted more than 4,000 new teens in 1997–1998 when it started. This ongoing program, which won a Highsmith Award for Excellence, succeeded partly because of community partnerships at the centers and local block grants (http://dallaslibrary.org/teenwise.htm).

Suffolk (New York) Public Library's cooperative library portal has pages just for kids and teens. However, the links go beyond fun and games—as well as online homework help—to include a separate page of information on bullying, trauma, cyber safety, special needs, and teen parenting (http://www.suffolk.lib.ny.us/youth/parenting.html#teen).

Redwood High School Library (Larkspur, California) has a bank of assistive technology systems for students with disabilities. Instructional aides are encouraged to bring their students into the library and work with them individually alongside other classes. Students with special needs are given highly structured instruction in the use of online databases. In addition, talking books and associated equipment are circulated for visually impaired and dyslexic students (http://redwood.org).

Trinity Valley School (Fort Worth, Texas) accommodates the visually impaired through large print, Braille, and recorded print materials, descriptive videos, and adaptive equipment. Their library Web portal provides teachers and parents with pertinent information, and the library staff work proactively with these students (http://faculty.trinityvalleyschool.org/library).

Long Beach (Long Beach, California) Public Library's Information Center for People with Disabilities provides assistive technologies as well as videos, large print materials, reference books, and more. Funding comes from the federal Library Services and Technology Act (http://www.lbpl.org).

These programs work because they have incorporated and supported several factors over a long period of time. They also focus on teens, and publicize their services accordingly; and many programs involved teens in the planning stages. Additionally, most of the programs involve partnerships outside the library, which provide a broader base of support. The classic study *Giving in America* (1975) lists the major benefits of community collaboration:

- initiatives: groups listen to their constituents and are not hampered by bureaucratic red tape
- public policy: groups can research issues independently and make informed decisions to governing bodies
- alternative advocacy: independent groups can support teen interest groups with fewer restrictions
- service safety net: government regulations insure that teens can get needed services, and independent groups can intervene when politics constrains certain interests such as religion
- citizenship: bipartisan groups can model and support teen civic activism

YOUR TURN

Now it is *your* turn to act. If you have done your homework, and established a good rapport with teens, then you can put your best intentions into action. Start with something concrete and doable that will result in positive change in a short period of time. Providing a low-end computer system or two for e-mail access, and offering workshops on how to get free accounts and use them, can be a worthwhile start.

The main idea is to take action and work with teens to help them feel good about themselves and empower them through the effective use of technology. Since the library is a community asset, working in concert with the rest of the community helps build a strong foundation for teen success. The Children's Partnership (2000) recommends the following action agenda for public and private sectors:

- prepare all young people for jobs and civic life
- assure that our schools equip young people to succeed
- put technology to work to help underserved communities

In the final analysis, teens are our greatest asset, and the future of each one will shape the role of libraries in the future.

WORKS CITED

The Children's Partnership. (2000). *Online content for low-income and underserved Americans*. Santa Monica, CA: The Children's Partnership. http://www.childrenspartnership.org/pub/low_income/index.html.

Commission on Private Philanthropy and Public Needs. (1975). *Giving in America: Toward a stronger voluntary sector: Report of the Commission on Private Philanthropy and Public Needs*. Washington, DC: The Commission on Private Philanthropy and Public Needs.

BIBLIOGRAPHY

Administration of Children & Families. (2002). *Profile of America's youth.* Washington, DC: U.S. Department of Health and Human Services. Retrieved November 25, 2004, from http://www.acf.hhs.gov/programs/fysb/youth info/profile.htm.

Adolescent Directory Online. http://education.indiana.edu/cas/adol/adol.html.

Ailworth, E. (2004, March 23). On the Web, Gen-Y and civic duty click. *Los Angeles Times,* E10.

Alire, C., & Archibeque, O. (1998). *Serving Latino communities.* New York: Neal-Schuman.

American Academy of Child and Adolescent Psychiatry. (2003). *Facts for families.* Washington, DC: American Academy of Child and Adolescent Psychiatry. Retrieved November 25, 2004, from http://www.aacap.org.

American Association of School Administrators. (2003). *Technology.* Arlington, VA: AASA. Retrieved November 25, 2004, from http://www.aasa.org/issues_and_insights/technology.

American Association of University Women. (2000). *Tech-savvy: Educating girls in the new computer age.* Washington, DC: AAUW.

American Library Association. (2003). *Library advocate's handbook.* (Spanish ed.) Chicago: American Library Association. Retrieved November 25, 2004, from http://www.ala.org/pio/libraryadvocateshandbookspanish.pdf.

American Library Association. (2002, June). Digital inclusion. *American Libraries, 33*(6), 50–57.

American Library Association. (2002, May). *Principles for the networked world.* Chicago: American Library Association.

American Library Association. (1999, August). Against all odds. *American Libraries, 30*(7). Issue.

American Library Association Social Responsibility Round Table. (1999). *Recommendations for action in implementing ALA's "Library services for the poor" resolution.* Chicago: American Library Association.

Ancess, J. (2003). *Beating the odds: High schools as communities of commitment.* New York: Teachers College Press.

Ansell, S., & Park, J. (2003, May 8). Tracking tech trends. *Education Week on the Web.* Retrieved November 25, 2004, from http://www.edweek.org.

Association of Educational Service Agencies. (2003, September). ESAs serving rural areas: Shrinking distances and compensating for size. *Perspectives, 9.* Retrieved November 25, 2004, from http://www.aaesa.org/Pubs/AESA%20PerspJournal%202003.pdf.

Athletes United for Peace. (2003). *Digital Technology Academy.* Washington, DC: Athletes United for Peace. http://www.athletesunitedforpeace.org/digital.html.

Atkins, Holly. (2003, January 20). The library's fresher than you think. *St. Petersburg Times.* St. Petersburg, Florida, 3D.

Attewell, P. (2001, July). The first and second digital divides. *Sociology of Education, 74*(3), 252–259.

Bard, T. (1999). *Student assistants in the school library media center.* Englewood, CO: Teacher Ideas Press.

Beilke, P., & Sciara, F. (1986). *Selecting materials for and about Hispanic and East Asian children and young people.* Hamden, CT: Shoestring Press.

Beloit College. (2003). *Beloit College mindset list.* Beloit, WI: Beloit College. Retrieved November 25, 2004, from http://www.beloit.edu/~pubaff/releases/2003/03mindsetlist.html.

Benard, B. (1995). *Fostering resilience in children.* ERIC Digest. Champaign, IL: ERIC Clearinghouse for Elementary and Early Childhood Education. (ERIC Document Reproduction Service No. ED386327).

Benson, C., & Christian, S. (Eds.). (2002). *Writing to make a difference.* New York: Teachers College Press.

Benton Foundation. Retrieved November 25, 2004, from http://www.benton.org.

Besharov, D. (Ed.). (1999). *America's disconnected youth.* Washington, DC: CWLA Press.

Bolt, D., & Crawford, R. (2000). *Digital divide: Computers and our children's future.* New York: TV Books.

Bowker, A. (2003). *Sisters in the blood: The education of women in Native America.* Washington, DC: Office of Educational Research and Improvement.

Braun, L. (2003). *Technically involved: Technology-based youth participation activities for your library*. Chicago: American Library Association.

Braun, L. (2002). *Teens.Library: Developing Internet services for young adults*. Chicago: American Library Association.

Bureau of Labor Statistics. (2004). *Tomorrow's jobs*. Washington, DC: U.S. Department of Labor.

Burgstahler, S. (1999, July). Technology and people with (dis)abilities. *CUE Newsletter 21*(4) 1, 23–25.

Burt, M., Resnick, G., & Novick, E. (1998). *Building supportive communities for at-risk adolescents*. Washington, DC: American Psychological Association.

Caine, R., & Caine, G. (1997). *Education on the edge of possibility*. Alexandria, VA: Association for Supervision and Curriculum Development.

Canadian Council on Social Development. (2000). *Immigrant youth in Canada: Lifestyle patterns of immigrant youth*. Ontario: Canadian Council on Social Development. Retrieved November 25, 2004, from http://www.ccsd.ca/subsites/cd/docs/iy.

Carlson, S. (2003, May 2). Firm's survey of college-bound students finds no digital divide among them. *The Chronicle of Higher Education*, 49(34), A37.

Carnegie Corporation of New York. (1995). *Great transitions: Preparing adolescents for a new century*. New York: Carnegie Corporation. Retrieved November 25, 2004, from http://www.carnegie.org/sub/pubs/reports/great_transitions/gr_intro.html.

Carr, M. (2003, August). The need for a national migrant student tracking database. Folsom, CA: Center for Digital Education. Retrieved November 25, 2004, from http://www.centerdigitaled.com/converge/?pg=magstory&id=65467.

Castellano, M., Stringfield, S., & Stone, J. (2003, Summer). Secondary career and technical education and comprehensive school reform: Implications for research and practice. *Review of Educational Research, 73*(2), 231–272.

Catholic Migrant Farmworker Network. (2003). *Education and child-care*. Boise, ID: Catholic Migrant Farmworker Network. Retrieved November 25, 2004, from http://www.cmfn.org/education.html.

Center for Children & Technology. (2002). *Projects*. Boston: Education Development Center. Retrieved November 25, 2004, from http://www.edc.org/CCT/imagination_place.

Center for Educational Technology in Indian America. Retrieved November 4, 2004, from http://www.4Directions.org.

Center for Information and Research on Civic Learning and Engagement. (2002). *Youth civic engagement*. Washington, DC: CIRCLE.

Center for Language Minority Education and Research. http://www.clmer.csulb.edu.

Center for Media Education. (2001). *Teensites.com: A field guide to the new digital landscape*. Washington, DC: Center for Media Education.

Center for Research on Parallel Computation. (2003). *Online educational resources.* Houston, TX: Rice University. Retrieved November 26, 2004, from http://hhse.cs.rice.edu/CRPC/education/resources.html.

Center for Universal Design. (1997). *What is universal design?* Raleigh, NC: North Carolina State University. Retrieved November 26, 2004, from http://www.design.ncsu.edu/cud/univ_design/princ_overview.htm.

Center for Women and Information Technology. (2003). *Girl-related resources.* Baltimore: University of Maryland, Baltimore County. Retrieved November 26, 2004, from http://www.umbc.edu/cwit/girlres.html.

CEO Forum on Education and Technology. (2001). *School technology and readiness report: Year 4 report.* Washington, DC: CEO Forum on Education and Technology. Retrieved November 26, 2004, from http://www.ceoforum.org/downloads/report4.pdf.

Chatman, E. (1996). The impoverished lifeworld of outsiders. *Journal of the American Society for Information Science, 47,* 193–206.

Chelton, M. (1998). Adult-adolescent services encounters: The library context. Doctoral dissertation. Brunswick, NJ: Rutgers. Dissertation Abstracts International 58(11), 4110. (UMINO. SAT 9814054). Abstract obtained from Dissertation Abstracts Online.

Child Trends DataBank. (2003). Teens. Washington, DC: Child Trends. Retrieved November 26, 2004, from http://www.childtrendsdatabank.org/search_age.cfm#TEENS.

Children, Youth, and Families At Risk Program. (2002). *Annual report.* Washington, DC: CYFAR. Retrieved November 26, 2004, from http://www.reeusda.gov/nea/family/cyfar/cyfar.html.

The Children's Partnership. (2003). *The search for high-quality online content for low-income and underserved communities: Evaluating and producing what's needed.* Santa Monica, CA: The Children's Partnership.

The Children's Partnership. (2000). *Online content for low-income and underserved Americans.* Santa Monica, CA: The Children's Partnership. Retrieved November 26, 2004, from http://www.childrenspartnership.org/pub/low_income/index.html.

Chu, C. (2000). *The digital divide: A resource list.* Los Angeles: UCLA. Retrieved November 26, 2004, from http://www.gseis.ucla.edu/faculty/chu/digdiv.

Clarke, A. (2002). *Social and emotional distress among American Indian and Alaska Native students: Research findings.* ERIC Digest. Charleston, WV: ERIC Clearinghouse on Rural Education and Small Schools. (ERIC Document Reproduction Service No. EDO-RC-01-11).

Commission on Private Philanthropy and Public Needs. (1975). *Giving in America: Toward a stronger voluntary sector: Report of the Commission on Private Philanthropy and Public Needs.* Washington, DC: The Commission on Private Philanthropy and Public Needs.

Community Technology Center. (2003). *Community Technology Centers' network.*

Cambridge, MA: CTC. Retrieved November 26, 2004, from http://shwww.ctcnet.org.

Community Technology Network of the Bay Area. (2003). *Information and computer literacy.* San Francisco, CA: Community Technology Network of the Bay Area. Retrieved November 26, 2004, from http://www.ctnbayarea.org/resources/curriculum/information_literacy.html.

Community Technology Review. Retrieved November 26, 2004, from http://www.comtechreview.org.

Compaine, B. (Ed.). (2001). *The digital divide: Facing a crisis or creating a myth?* Cambridge, MA: MIT Press.

ConnectNet/Conectado Campaign. (2003). Washington, DC: Kaiser Family Foundation. Retrieved November 26, 2004, from http://www.kff.org/mediapartnerships/20010326a-index.cfm.

Constantino, R. (Ed.). (1998). *Literacy, access, and libraries among the language minority population.* Lanham, MD: Scarecrow Press.

Cravens, J. (2002). *Tip sheets.* Austin, TX: Coyote Communications. Retrieved November 26, 2004, from http://www.coyotecommunications.com.

DeBell, M., & Chapman, C. (2003). *Computer and Internet use by children and adolescents in 2001.* Washington, DC: National Center for Educational Statistics. Retrieved November 26, 2004, from http://nces.ed.gov/pubsearch/pubsinfo.asp?pubid=2004014.

Digital Abiquiu. (2003). *Northern New Mexico local directory.* Sante Fe, NM: Digital Abiquiu. Retrieved November 26, 2004, from http://digitalabiquiu.com/pages/local/nmlocaldirectory.html.

Doherty, C. (2002, September). Extending horizons: Critical technological literacy for urban Aboriginal students. *Journal of Adolescent & Adult Literacy, 46*(1), 50–59.

Dooling, J. (2000, October). What students want to learn about computers. *Educational Leadership, 58*(2), 20–24.

Durrance, J., & Fisher, K. (2003). Determining how libraries and librarians help. *Library Trends, 51*(4), 541–570.

Educational Testing Service. (2003). *Parsing the achievement gap: Baselines for tracking progress.* Princeton, NJ: ETS.

Eisenman, R. (1993). Characteristics of adolescent felons in a prison treatment program. *Adolescence, 28*(111), 695–699.

Evans, G. (2004, February). The environment of childhood poverty. *American Psychologist, 59*(2), 77–92.

Farmer, L. (2001). *Teaming with opportunity: Media programs, community constituencies, and technology.* Englewood, CO: Libraries Unlimited.

Farmer, L. (2001, January). Building information literacy through a whole school reform approach. *Knowledge Quest, 29,* 20–24.

Farmer, L. (1997). *Training student library staff.* Worthington, OH: Linworth.

Farmer, L. (1994). *Leadership within the school library and beyond.* Worthington, OH: Linworth.

Fisher, J., & Hill, A. (2003, November). Reading in the cyber age: Getting teens wired to read! *Library Media Connection, 22*(3), 23–25.

Forum Focus. (2003, September). Community partnerships for learning: Blurring the lines. *Youth Today, 1*(2), 29–31.

Frechette, J. (2002). *Developing media literacy in cyberspace: Pedagogy and critical learning for the 21st century classroom.* Westport, CT: Praeger.

Freeman, David, & Freeman, Yvonne. (1998). *Successful strategies for teaching ELD.* Covina, CA: California Association for Bilingual Education.

From digital divide to digital opportunity; Community technology centers: Making a difference in communities across the nation. (2000). Washington, DC: White House. Retrieved November 26, 2004, from http://clinton3.nara.gov/WH/New/digitaldivide/digital5.html.

Gambone, M., Klem, A., & Connell, J. (2002). *Finding out what matters for youth: Testing key links in a community action framework for youth development.* Philadelphia: Youth Development Strategies.

Gender & Diversities Institute. (2003). *Technology and gender projects.* Newton, MA: Education Development Center. Retrieved November 26, 2004, from http://www.edc.org/GDI/about.htm.

Gimpel, J., Lay, J., & Schuknecht, J. (2003). *Cultivating democracy: Civic environments and political socialization in America.* Washington, DC: Brookings Institution Press.

Ginorio, Angela, & Huston, Michelle. (2000). *Â¡sí, se puede! Yes, we can: Latinas in school.* Washington, DC: American Association of University Women. Retrieved November 26, 2004, from http://www.aauw.org/research/latina.cfm.

Girls in Technology. Washington, DC: Women in Technology. Retrieved November 26, 2004, from http://www.girlsintechnology.org/index.html.

Goad, T. (2002). *Information literacy and workplace performance.* Westport, CT: Quorum Books.

Gordon, H., & Herz, J. (2001). *Digital divide and libraries: Services.* Sacramento: California State University, Sacramento.

Grant, R., & Wong, S. (2003, February). Barriers to literacy for language-minority learners: An argument for change in the literacy education profession. *Journal of Adolescent & Adult Literacy, 46*(5), 386–393.

Greene, G., & Kochhar-Bryant, C. (2003). *Pathways to successful transition for youth with disabilities.* Upper Saddle River, NJ: Merrill.

Guerena, S. (Ed.). (2000). *Library services to Latinos: An anthology.* Jefferson, NC: McFarland.

Hackbarth, S. (2001, April). Changes in primary students' computer literacy as a function of classroom use and gender. *TechTrends, 45*(4), 19–27.

Harvard Graduate School of Education. (2003). *85 percent of immigrant children experience separations during migration.* Cambridge, MA: Harvard University. Retrieved November 26, 2004, from http://gseweb.harvard.edu/news/features/suarez06292001.html.

Haveman, R., & Wolf, B. (1994). *Succeeding generations: On the effects of investment in children.* New York: Russell Sage Foundation.

HeavyRunner, I., & Morris, J. (1997). Traditional native culture and resilience. *Research Practice, 5*(1).

Hernandez, A. (2002, December). *Can education play a role in the prevention of youth gangs in Indian country? One tribe's approach.* ERIC Digest. Charleston, WV: ERIC Clearinghouse on Rural Education and Small Schools. (ERIC Document Reproduction Service No. EDO-RC-02-12).

Hersch, P. (1999). *A tribe apart: A journey into the heart of American adolescence.* New York: Ballantine.

Hillabrant, W., Romano, M., Stang, D., & Charleston, G. M. (1991). *Native American education at a turning point: Current demographics and trends.* Washington, DC: U.S. Department of Education. Indian Nations at Risk Task Force. (ERIC Document Reproduction Service No. ED343756).

Hispanic Research Center. (2003). *Digital divide solutions.* Phoenix, AZ: Arizona State University. Retrieved November 26, 2004, from http://www.asu.edu/DigitalDivideSolutions.

Holloway, J. (2003, September). Managing culturally diverse classrooms. *Educational Leadership, 61*(1), 90–91.

Howe, N., & Strauss, W. (2000). *Millennials rising.* New York: Vintage.

Howley, A., & Pendarvis, E. (2002, December). *Recruiting and retaining rural school administrators.* ERIC Digest. Charleston, WV: ERIC Clearinghouse on Rural Education and Small Schools. (ERIC Document Reproduction Service No. EDO-RC-02-7).

Huang, G. (2002, December). What federal statistics reveal about migrant farmworkers: A summary for education. ERIC Digest. Charleston, WV: ERIC Clearinghouse on Rural Education and Small Schools. (ERIC Document Reproduction Service No. EDO-RD-02-9).

Hull, G., & Schultz, K. (Eds.). (2002). *School's out: Bridging out-of-school literacies with classroom practice.* New York: Teachers College Press.

Hutchinson, N. (2001, June). Beyond ADA compliance: Redefining accessibility. *American Libraries, 32*(6), 76–78.

Immroch, B., & McCook, K. (Eds.). (2000). *Library services to youth of Hispanic heritage.* Jefferson, NC: McFarland.

Institute for Women and Technology. (2002). *Changing the world for women and for technology.* Palo Alto, CA: Institute for Women and Technology. Retrieved November 26, 2004, from http://www.iwt.org/home.html.

Irvine, J. (1990). *Black students and school failure: Policies, practices, and prescriptions.* Westport, CT: Greenwood.

Ishizuka, K. (2004, July). A Texas district goes digital. *School Library Journal, 50*(7), 14.

Jackson, M. (2003, October). Now what. *Working Mother, 28*(9) 41–51.

Jacobsonk, J. (2003, Fall). Second language literacy development: From theory to practice. *California Reader, 37*(1), 12–16.

James, C. (1974). *Beyond custom.* New York: Agathon Press.

Joint Venture. (2003). *Community technology resources.* San Jose CA: Joint Venture. Retrieved November 26, 2004, from http://www.jointventure.org/programs-initiatives/smartvalley/resources.html.

Jonassen, D. (Ed.). (2003). *Handbook of research on educational communications and technology.* Mahwah, NJ: Lawrence Erlbaum.

Jones, J. (2003). *Helping teens cope: Resources for school library media specialists and other youth workers.* Worthington, OH: Linworth.

Jones, P., & Pfeil, A. (2004, Spring). Public library YA Web pages for the twenty-first century. *YALS,* 14–18.

Joseph, B., & Klein, R. (2002). *Surfing alone: Lesson from the global kids' digital divide survey.* New York: Global Kids. Retrieved November 26, 2004, from http://www.globalkids.org.

Josey, E., & DeLoach, M. (Eds.). (2003). *Handbook of Black librarianship.* Lanham, MD: Scarecrow.

Kapitzke, C., et al. (2000). Weaving words with the Dreamweaver: Literacy, indigeneity, and technology. *Journal of Adolescent & Adult Literacy, 44,* 336–355.

Katz, J., & Rice, R. (2002). *Social consequences & Internet use: Access, involvement, and interaction.* Cambridge, MA: MIT Press.

Katz, J., Rice, R., & Aspden, P. (2001, November). The Internet, 1995–2000: Access, civic involvement, and social interaction. *American Behavioral Scientist, 45*(3), 405–419.

Keeble, L., & Loader, B. (2001). *Social capital and cyberpower.* London: Routledge.

Kidsnet. (2003). *Kidsnet media news.* Washington, DC: Kidsnet. Retrieved November 26, 2004, from http://www.kidsnet.org.

Kleiner, A., & Lewis, L. (2003). *Internet access in U.S. public schools and classrooms: 1994–2002.* Washington, DC: National Center for Educational Statistics. Retrieved November 26, 2004, from http://nces.ed.gov/pubsearch/pubsinfo.asp?pubid=2004011.

Kling, R. (2000). Learning about information technologies and social change: The contribution of social informatics. *Information Society, 16,* 217–232.

Kunzman, R. (2002, May). Extracurricular activities. *Knowledge Quest, 30*(5), 22–25.

Kuttan, A., & Peters, L. (2003). *From digital divide to digital opportunity.* Lanham, MD: Scarecrow Press.

Lau, J., & Lazarus, W. (2002). *Pathways to our future: A multimedia training program that works for youth.* Santa Monica, CA: Children's Partnership. Retrieved November 26, 2004, from http://www.cctpg.org/workforce/pathways-report.pdf.

Lazarus, W., & Lipper, L. (2000, July). Creating a children's policy agenda in the digital world. *Next Generation Reports,* 1–4.

Lee, C. (Ed.). (2003, June). Reconceptualizing race and ethnicity in educational research. *Educational Researcher, 32*(5). Issue.

Lee, F., & Adams, N. (2001). *The digital divide: What have we done? What have we learned?* Washington, DC: CYFAR.

Lee, V., & Burkam, D. (2003, September). Dropping out of high school: The role of school organization and structure. *American Educational Research Journal, 40*(2), 353–393.

Lenhart, A. (2003). *The ever-shifting Internet population: A new look at Internet access and the digital divide.* Washington, DC: The Pew Internet and American Life Project. Retrieved November 26, 2004, from http://www.pewinternet.org/pdfs/PIP_Shifting_Net_Pop_Report.pdf.

Leonardo, Z. (2003). *Ideology, discourse, and school reform.* Westport, CT: Praeger.

Lerner, J., & Lerner, R. (Eds.). (2001). *Adolescence in America: An encyclopedia.* Santa Barbara, CA: ABC-CLIO.

Levine, F., & Rosich, K. (1996). *Social causes of violence: Crafting a science agenda.* Washington, DC: American Sociological Association.

Light, Jane. (2001). *Bridging the digital divide.* Washington, DC: CNN. Retrieved November 26, 2004, from http://www.cnn.com/SPECIALS/2000/virtualvillages/story/essays/light.

LINCT Coalition. (2001). *Learn and earn: Bridging the divides that disenfranchise.* Hampton Bays, NY: EPIE Institute. Retrieved November 26, 2004, from http://linct.org.

Loertscher, D., & Woolls, B. (2002, May). Teenage users of libraries. *Knowledge Quest, 30*(5), 31–36.

Lonergan, J. (2001). Preparing urban teachers to use technology for instruction. ERIC Digest. New York: ERIC Clearinghouse on Urban Education. (ERIC Document Reproduction Service No. ED460190).

Lonergan, J. (2000). Internet access and content for urban schools and communities. ERIC Digest. New York: ERIC Clearinghouse on Urban Education. (ERIC Document Reproduction Service No. ED446180).

Luevano-Molina, S. (Ed.). (2001). *Immigrant politics and the public library.* Westport, CT: Greenwood.

Male, M. (2002). *Technology for inclusion: Meeting the special needs of all students.* Boston: Allyn & Bacon.

Maslow, A. (1962). *Toward a psychology of being.* Princeton, NJ: Van Nostrand.

McCabe, R. (2001). *Civic librarianship: Renewing the social mission of the public library.* Lanham, MD: Scarecrow Press.

McCook, K. (Ed.). (2000, May). Reaching out to poor people. *American Libraries, 31*(5), 45–58.

McDowell, S., & Strover, S. (2003). Setting the agenda for rural broadband. *Government Information Quarterly, 20*(2).

McNabb, M., et al. (1999). *Technology connections for school improvement planner's handbook.* Naperville, IL: North Central Regional Educational Laboratory.

Meganmarie. (2004). *Raising girls.* Fairfield, PA: Suite101.com. Retrieved November 26, 2004, from http://www.suite101.com/links.cfm/raising_girls.

Melecio, R., & Hanley, T. (2002, December). *Identification and recruitment of migrant students: Strategies and resources.* ERIC Digest. Charleston, WV: ERIC Clearinghouse on Rural Education and Small Schools. (ERIC Reproduction Document Service No. EDO-RC-02-10).

Merritt, S. (2002). The millennials: A perspective on America's next generation and their impact on higher education. PACAC Annual Conference, Seven Springs, PA, July 1.

Mestre, L. (2000, May). Improving computer-use success for students of diverse backgrounds. *Knowledge Quest, 28*(5), 20–28.

Meyers, E. (1999). The coolness factor: Ten libraries listen to youth. *American Libraries, 30*(10), 42–45.

MiddleWeb. (2003). *Schools, parents and communities working together.* Retrieved November 26, 2004, from http://www.middleweb.com/mw/resources/MWRpublic.html.

Minkel, W. (2004, July). As good as new: Recycled computers are a boon to cash-strapped schools. *School Library Journal, 50*(7), 27.

Moller, S. (2001). *Library service to Spanish speaking patrons: A practical guide.* Englewood, CO: Libraries Unlimited.

Molz, R., & Dain, P. (1999). *Civic space/cyberspace: The American public library in the information age.* Cambridge, MA: MIT.

Moore, E., et al. (2002). *It's working: People from low-income families disproportionately use library computers.* Seattle, WA: University of Washington.

Moore, E., Gordon, A., & Gordon, M. (2001). *Teens and public access computing in libraries.* Seattle: University of Washington. Retrieved November 26, 2004, from http://www.gatesfoundation.org/NR/Downloads/libraries/eval_docs/pdf/TeenReport.PDF.

Muhammad, T. (1998, March). About this issue. *Black Enterprise,* 13.

Murray, C. (2004, April). Students see tech as necessity, say schools fall short. *eSchool News,* 26.

National Association of Counties. (1999). *The face of homelessness.* Washington, DC: National Association of Counties.

National Center for Education Statistics. (2003). *Computer and Internet use by children and adolescents in 2001.* Washington, DC: National Center for Education Statistics.

National Center for Education Statistics. (2003a). *Internet access in U.S. public schools and classrooms: 1994–2001.* Washington, DC: National Center for Education Statistics.

National Center for Education Statistics. (2003b). *School and staff survey, 1999–2000.* Washington, DC: National Center for Education Statistics.

National Center for Education Statistics. (2003c). *Technology in schools: Suggestions, tools and guidelines for assessing elementary and secondary education.* Washington, DC: National Center for Education Statistics.

National Council on Disability. (2001). The accessible future. Washington, DC: U.S. Department of Education. Retrieved November 26, 2004, from http://www.ncd.gov/newsroom/publications/2001/pdf/accessiblefuture.html.

National Institute for Community Innovations. (2001). The digital equity toolkit. Washington, DC: NICI. Retrieved November 26, 2004, from http://www.nici-mc2.org/de_toolkit/pages/toolkit.htm.

National School Boards Foundation. (2003). *Safe & smart*. Alexandria, VA: National School Boards Foundation.

National Telecommunications and Information Administration. (1999). *Falling through the Net: Defining the digital divide*. Washington, DC: U.S. Department of Commerce. Retrieved November 26, 2004, from http://www.ntia.doc.gov/ntiahome/fttn99/contents.html.

Norris, P. (2001). *Digital divide: Civic engagement, information poverty, and the Internet worldwide*. Cambridge, MA: Cambridge University Press.

Novak, T., & Hoffman, D. (1997). *Diversity on the Internet: The relationship to race to access and usage*. Paper prepared for the Aspen Institute's Forum on Diversity and the Media, Queenstown, Maryland, November 5–7.

O'Dell, K. (2002). *Library materials and services for teen girls*. Westport, CT: Libraries Unlimited.

O'Hare, W., & Mather, M. (2003). *The growing number of kids in severely distressed neighborhoods: Evidence from the 2000 census*. Baltimore, MD: Annie E. Casey Foundation.

Otterbourg, S. (2000). *Investing in partnerships for student success: A basic tool for community stakeholders to guide educational partnership, development, and management*. Washington, DC: Partnership for Family Involvement in Education. Retrieved November 26, 2004, from http://www.ed.gov/pubs/investpartner/index.html.

Partnership for 21st Century Skills. Retrieved November 28, 2004, from http://www.21stcenturyskills.org.

Peasley, B. (2002, June). It takes a virtual village to empower all the villagers. *American Libraries, 33*(6), 54–56.

Phelan, P., Davidson, A., & Yu, H. (1998). *Adolescents' worlds: Negotiating family, peers, and school*. New York: Teachers College Press.

PowerUp. Retrieved November 26, 2004, from http://www.power-up.net.

Public Broadcasting System. (2003). *Digital divide*. Washington, DC: PBS. Retrieved November 28, 2004, from http://www.pbs.org/digitaldivide.

Public/Private Ventures. (2000). *Youth development: Issues, challenges, and directions*. Philadelphia, PA: P/PV. Retrieved November 26, 2004, from http://www.ppv.org/content/reports/ydv_pdf.html.

Raffoul, P., & McNeece, C. (Eds.). (1996). *Future issues of social work practice*. Boston: Allyn & Bacon.

Reid, K., & Mediatore, K. (2003, Fall). The 411 is now the shiznet. *YALS*, 7–9.

Reinking, M., et al. (Eds.). (1998). *Handbook of literacy and technology*. Mahwah, NJ: Erlbaum.

Rice, F. (1998). *The adolescent: Development, relationships, and culture*. (9th ed.). Boston: Allyn & Bacon.

Rosen, D. (1998). *Driver education for the information superhighway*. Washington, DC:

National Institute for Literacy. Retrieved November 28, 2004, from http://courses.unt.edu/mewilcox/drivers_ed_for_the_internet.

San Jose State University. School of Library and Information Science. (2003). *Advocacy for school library media teachers*. San Jose, CA: SJSU. Retrieved November 26, 2004, from http://witloof.sjsu.edu/proj/advocacy.

Schmar-Dobler, E. (2003, September). Reading on the Internet: The link between literacy and technology. *Journal of Adolescent & Adult Literacy, 47*(1), 80–85.

Secretary's Commission on Achieving Necessary Skills. (1991). *What work requires of schools: A SCANS report for America 2000*. Washington, DC: Department of Labor.

Servon, L. (2002). *Bridging the digital divide: Technology, community, and public policy.* Oxford: Blackwell.

Silverman, S., & Pritchard, A. (1999, September). Building their future: Girls and technology education in Connecticut. *Journal of Technology Education, 7*(2). Retrieved November 26, 2004, from http://scholar.lib.vt.edu/ejournals/JTE/v7n2/silverman.jte-v7n2.htm.

Simpson, R. (2001). *Raising teens: A synthesis of research and a foundation for action.* Boston: Harvard Center for Health Communication.

Solomon, G., Allen, N., & Resta, R. (Eds.). (2003). *Toward a digital divide: Bridging the divide in education.* Boston: Allyn & Bacon.

Staresina, L. (2003, July 10). Technology in Education. *Education Week on the Web*. Retrieved November 26, 2004, from http://www.edweek.org/context/topics/issuespage.cfm?id=96.

Strand, J., & Peacock, T. (2002, December). *Nurturing resilience and school success for American Indian and Alaska native students.* ERIC Digest. Charleston, WV: ERIC Clearinghouse on Rural Education and Small Schools. (ERIC Document Reproduction Service No. EDO-RC-02-11).

Strang, W., von Glatz, A., & Hammer, P. (2002, December). Setting the agenda: Native American and Alaska native education research priorities. ERIC Digest. Charleston, WV: ERIC Clearinghouse on Rural Education and Small Schools. (ERIC Document Reproduction Service No. EDO-RC-02-14).

Strate, L., Jacobson, J., & Gibson, S. (Eds.). (2003). *Communication and cyberspace: Social interaction in an electronic environment.* (2nd ed.). Cresskill, NJ: Hampton Press.

Sullivan, D. (2003, September 2). Search engine size. SearchEngineWatch.com. Retrieved November 26, 2004, from http://www.searchenginewatch.com/reports/sizes.html.

Tatum, A. (2003, May). All degreed up and nowhere to go: Black males and literacy education. *Journal of Adolescent & Adult Literacy, 46*(8), 620–623.

Taylor, R., & McAtee, R. (2003, March). Turning a new page to life and literacy. *Journal of Adolescent & Adult Literacy, 46*(6), 476–481.

TechLearning. Retrieved November 26, 2004, from http://techLEARNING.com.

Technology Counts 2001. (2001, May 10). *Education Week.*

Teitelbaum, P., & Kaufman, P. (2002). *Labor Market Outcomes of Non-College-Bound High School Graduates*. Washington, DC: U.S. Department of Education (NCES 2002–126).

Thomases, J. (2003, September). Voices from the fields. *Youth Today, 1*(2), 3–4.

UNICEF. (2003). *Girls' education: Focus on technology*. New York: UNICEF.

United Neighborhood Houses of New York. (2002). *Technology for learning*. New York: United Neighborhood Houses of New York. Retrieved November 26, 2004, from http://www.unhny.org/technology/tech_for_learning.cfm.

University of California, Berkeley. School of Information Management and Systems. (2003). *How much information?* Berkeley, CA: University of California, Berkeley. Retrieved November 26, 2004, from http://www.sims.berkeley.edu/research/projects/how-much-info/internet.html.

U.S. Department of Commerce. (2002). *A nation online: How Americans are expanding their use of the Internet*. Washington, DC: U.S. Department of Commerce. Retrieved November 26, 2004, from http://www.ntia.doc.gov/ntiahome/dn/.

U.S. Department of Commerce. (n.d.). *How access benefits children: Connecting our kids to the world of information*. Washington, DC: U.S. Department of Commerce. Retrieved November 26, 2004, from http://www.ntia.doc.gov/otiahome/top/publicationmedia/How_ABC/How_ABC.html.

U.S. Department of Education Office of Educational Technology. (2003). *Tool kit for bridging the digital divide in your community*. Washington, DC: U.S. Department of Education. Retrieved November 26, 2004, from http://www.ed.gov/Technology/tool_kit.html.

U.S. Department of Health, Education and Welfare. (1977). *Federal policy on education and work*. Washington, DC: Government Printing Office.

Varlas, L. (2003, September). The heart of the city: Teacher leadership in urban schools. *Education Update, 54*(6), 1–8.

Venturella, K. (1998). *Poor people and library services*. Jefferson, NC: McFarland.

Viadero, E. (2003, November 26). Study probes factors fueling achievement gaps. *Education Week, 23*(13), 1, 12.

Warren-Sams, Barbara. (1997). *Closing the equity gap in technology access and use: A practical guide for K-12 educators*. Portland, OR: Northwest Regional Educational Laboratory.

Warschauer, M. (2003). *Technology and social inclusion: Rethinking the digital divide*. Cambridge, MA: MIT Press.

Watson, B. (2002). *Community change for youth development: Ten lessons from the CCYD initiative*. Philadelphia: Public/Private Ventures. Retrieved November 26, 2004, from http://www.ppv.org/content/reports/ten%20lessons.htm.

Wehmeyer, M., et al. (2003). *Theory in self-determination: Foundations for educational practice*. Springfield, IL: Charles Thomas.

Wessler, S. (2003, September). It's hard to learn when you're scared. *Educational Leadership, 61*(1), 40–43.

Wiles, J., & Bondi, J. (1993). *An exemplary middle school.* Upper Saddle River, NJ: Merrill-Prentice Hall.

Wilhelm, A. (2001, April). They threw me a computer . . . but what I really needed was a life preserver. *First Monday, 6*(4). Retrieved November 26, 2004, from http://firstmonday.org/issues/issue6_4/wilhelm/index.html.

Wilhelm, T., Carmen, D., & Reynolds, M. (2002). *Connecting kids to technology: Challenges and opportunities.* Baltimore, MD: Annie E. Casey Foundation. Retrieved November 28, 2004, from http://www.aypf.org/forumbriefs/2002/fb071802.htm.

Williams-Boyd, P. (Ed.). (2003). *Middle grades education.* Santa Barbara, CA: ABC-CLIO.

Young Adult Library Services Association. (2003). *Young adults deserve the best: Competencies for librarians serving youth.* Chicago: American Library Association. Retrieved November 26, 2004, from http://www.ala.org/ala/yalsa/profdev/youngadultsdeserve.htm.

Youth Learn. (2003). *Connecting youth to a brighter future.* Education Development Center. Retrieved November 26, 2004, from http://youthlearn.org.

Yuhip. Retrieved November 26, 2004, from http://www.yuhip.org.

Zollo, P. (1999). *Wise up to teens: Insights into marketing and advertising to teenagers.* (2nd ed.). Ithaca, NY: New Strategist.

Zuvekas, A., et al. (1999). *Mini environment assessment of the health status and needs of the poor.* Washington, DC: George Washington University.

INDEX

About the Author

LESLEY S. J. FARMER, Professor, Library Media Technology, California State University, Long Beach, is author of more than a dozen professional books for librarians. She has worked in all types of libraries, particularly in school settings and also trains educators in educational technology.